VOLUME 59   JANUARY 2008   PAGES 1–150

Living with Stalin's Ghost

*A Fulbright Memoir
of Moscow and the New Russia*

BY

BRUCE C. DANIELS

TRANSACTIONS
THE CONNECTICUT ACADEMY OF ARTS AND SCIENCES

P.O. Box 208211
New Haven, Connecticut 06520-8211

CAAS@YALE.EDU

© 2008 by the Connecticut Academy of Arts and Sciences

Published by the Connecticut Academy of Arts and Sciences,
P.O. Box 208211, New Haven, Connecticut 06520-8211.

Printed in the United States of America.

The paper used in this publication meets the minimum requirements
of American National Standard for Information Services—
Permanence of Paper for Printed Library Materials,
ANSI z39.48–1984. ∞

This book was composed in New Baskerville, an Adobe Systems digital
typeface based on Baskerville, the English transitional typeface designed
by John Baskerville in the mid-18th century.

Typography and design by Quicksilver Communication,
Hamden, Connecticut.
Printing and binding by Thomson-Shore, Inc., Dexter, Michigan.

Library of Congress Cataloging-in-Publication Data

Daniels, Bruce Colin.
 Living with Stalin's ghost : a Fulbright memoir of Moscow and the new
Russia by Bruce C. Daniels.
    p. cm. – (Transactions of The Connecticut Academy of Arts and Sci-
ences ; 59)
 ISBN 978-1-878508-27-0 (pbk. : alk. paper)
 1. Moscow (Russia)–Description and travel. 2. Russia (Federation)–
Social life and customs. 3. Daniels, Bruce Colin–Travel–Russia (Federa-
tion)–Moscow. I. Title. II. Series.

DK601.2.D36 2008
947.086--dc22

                                        2008000511

With love to
My daughters, Elizabeth, Abigail, and Nora
My sons-in-law, Pat and Rolando
My grandchildren, Patrick, Kate, and James

Table of Contents

About the Author

BRUCE C. DANIELS is the Gilbert M. Denman Endowed Professor of American History at the University of Texas at San Antonio. In 2005, he was the Nicolay Sivachev Fulbright Chair of History at Moscow State University. Before then, Daniels served as chair of the Department of History at Texas Tech University (2001-2004) and taught at the University of Winnipeg (1970-2001). He is author of several books, including *The Connecticut Town: Growth and Development, 1635-1790* (1979) and *Puritans at Play: Leisure and Recreation in Colonial New England* (1995, 1996).

Daniels previously contributed to the Memoir Series of The Connecticut Academy of Arts and Sciences in Memoir XXVII, *Voices of the New Republic: Connecticut Towns 1800-1832, Volume II: What We Think,* with an essay titled "The Remarkable Complexity of the Simple New England Town."

A former Peace Corps volunteer (Bihar, India, 1964-65) and Fulbright scholar (Duke University, 1993-94), Daniels also served as editor of the *Canadian Review of American Studies* (1978-86) and president of the Canadian Association for American Studies (1991-93). In 1996, Daniels was a candidate for the Democratic party's presidential nomination in the New Hampshire primary where he finished 7th in a field of 22 Democratic candidates.

Acknowledgments

Although I have poured my best efforts and much time into other books I have written, none of them has been very personal. This book is. Because it was originally written for family and friends, I have allowed my personal feelings, habits, commitments, and quirks to appear on many pages. This book also is intended to be a serious academic contribution to knowledge. It is a memoir written by a father and tourist but also an analysis of Russian society and politics written by a historian and Fulbright scholar.

It may appear ironic, therefore, that in such a personal book, I wish to thank institutions as much as individuals. Without these institutions and the dedicated people who serve them, however, I would never have been placed in the extraordinary position that allowed me to comment on a subject so distant from my usual scholarship.

The Fulbright Program is a national treasure for Americans and an international treasure for the citizens of the 140 countries around the world who participate in it. No other institution serves the cause of peace and promotes good will, education, and cultural understanding as wonderfully without a trace of partisan rancor. Nearly as remarkably, the Fulbright organization is efficiently administered and a joy to work with. I am proud to be a Fulbrighter and will always be grateful for having been given the privilege.

At the time I went to Moscow, I was teaching at Texas Tech University, which gave me a development leave and generous financial support. In particular I wish to thank the Department of History, the Provost's and President's offices, and especially Vice Provost Jim Brink, who arranged the leave so expeditiously.

I mention many of my colleagues and students at Moscow State University in the text of this book, but I wish to thank the university itself and the dozens of people there who so kindly and graciously welcomed me into their lives. Virtually every one of my twenty students accompanied me on outings around Moscow and befriended me as we were educating each other.

Since returning to the United States, I have taken a new job at the University of Texas at San Antonio. At UTSA, I wish to thank Dean Dan Gelo of the College of Liberal and Fine Arts for generously providing the Connecticut Academy of Arts and Sciences with a subvention towards the cost of publication. I also wish to thank Jack Reynolds, chair of the Department of History, who worked to make my move here so smooth that I have had time to polish this manuscript into publishable form.

I am also honored to have my memoir published by such a distinguished learned society as the Connecticut Academy of Arts and Sciences, and I wish to thank especially Sandra Rux, publications director, for encouraging me to submit the manuscript to the academy, and Carolyn Cooper, a member of the academy, for her considerable editorial help.

If my memoir has merit, two earlier institutions – the University of Connecticut, where I attended graduate school, and the University of Winnipeg, where I spent most of my teaching career – deserve the credit for transforming me from an apprentice to a professional scholar. I wish to thank the two people who symbolize these universities to me: Professor Fred Cazel, Jr., my advisor at Connecticut, and President Emeritus Henry E. Duckworth of Winnipeg.

Let me also thank a few friends and family who read this memoir as a manuscript and thought it worthy of publication: Robert and Kathryn Young, and Daniel Stone of Winnipeg; Alwyn and Nancy Barr, Paul and Ellen Carlson, and Penny Denison of Lubbock; and Abigail Daniels of West Hartford, Connecticut.

And finally, I wish to thank the following people for being important parts of my life: Mark Baldwin, Don Bailey, Hinton and Diana Bradbury, Dayle Everatt, Judith Graham, Hugh Grant and the Grant-Me-A-Champion Stable, Curt Hitchcox, John Ifkovic, Carolina Springett, Gordon McKinnon and Lori Spivak, Sarah McKinnon, and the Riccio family.

San Antonio, Texas
September 11, 2007

From Communist Russia to Capitalist Russia
The Enormity of Privatization

What did a country boy from New Hampshire, who turned Canadian and now teaches American history in Texas, know about Russia before he left to be a visiting professor at Moscow State University? Truth be told, not much. I knew enough to have passed and taught the basic Western Civilization history courses, I had read the newspaper and watched the evening news through forty years of the Cold War, and I had taken a two-week inland boat tour from Moscow to St. Petersburg in 1993, but that was just about the sum total of my expertise when I embarked on this adventure. I know that pleading ignorance is not necessarily a virtue, but honesty is, and I start this memoir of life in the new Russia by confessing how little I knew about life in the old Russia on the eve of my departure for Moscow, where I had the privilege of teaching as a Fulbright scholar.

In a strange way my lack of previous knowledge might be this commentary's greatest strength because I believe that I looked at my subject – Moscow in the twenty-first century – through the same uninformed eyes that my friends in New England, Winnipeg, and Texas would have if they had been as fortunate as I. Historically, Russians and Americans have not known much about each other. Despite a wary but successful World War Two partnership and a half-century of terrifying nuclear stalemate that also ended somewhat successfully – or at least not tragically – the ignorance remains and is further clouded by fear and suspicion. I used my stay in Moscow to learn as much as a novice could absorb in a short time and have tried to put it into a form that would allow other novices to share my journey.

In addition to not being a Russian historian, I am no Tocqueville or Twain. Thus I started this commentary with the modest goals of writing a guide to Russia for my family. I have never owned a camera and hence have never brought back pictures from any trip; instead I prefer to write about what I see. Somewhere along the way, while I was making my literary version of a family snapshot, I began to feel that it might be worth sharing with a wider audience. Nevertheless, I have kept the narrative personal, and it moves back and forth between the present and past tenses at times as if I were informally talking to people.

A NOTE ON PRIVATIZATION

When I had almost finished my commentary, I decided to insert this prefatory note on the privatization of the Russian economy at the beginning. By the time I ended my story, I had come to believe that the process of transforming Russia from a public to a private economy shaped every part of the Moscow that I described – even the tiniest details of daily life. Hence, a brief introduction to the privatization process will give the pages that follow more meaning.

Imagine, if you will, a United States and a Canada in which every significant piece of property and economic capital is owned by the government: all businesses, houses, apartments, factories, farms – from the corner grocery store to the newsstand to the café to the one-room efficiency suite to the coal mines to the sports teams to the aluminum smelter – everything is owned by the government. Imagine also a United States and a Canada where all people work for and are paid by the government: the waiter, the checkout clerk, the farmhand, the taxi driver, the hair stylist, the miner, the plumber, the news reporter, the professor, the lawyer, and the doctor – everyone is an employee of the state. And, finally, imagine a United States and a Canada with virtually no advertising for consumer goods, no foreign investment, no stock market, no stock ownership, no billboards, no store signs and no movies, television, or books that are not approved and distributed by the government.

For me, as for any American or Canadian, the enormous reality of a completely public economy is almost more than my mind can absorb. Now as you and I are reeling from our vague comprehension of what life would be like in a world where everything was owned by the government, and everyone worked for the government, try to imagine something else that may be yet more difficult. Imagine that the government abruptly announced that within a short period of fifteen to twenty years, the ownership of most of these public goods would be transferred to the private sector. From your small apartment to the local restaurant to the huge factories – most things would become the property of the people of the country, and the government would retain ownership of only those selected parts of the economy and the country's assets such as the military and necessary public infrastructure as it does in the United States and Canada. Most government employees would now become private service providers, entrepreneurs, or employees of private business. Stock markets could be opened, foreign investors and banks welcomed, foreign stores invited to set up shop and sell any goods that people wanted to buy. Local citizens and foreign nationals would be told that a country with many of the world's largest reserves of all sorts of natural resources now wanted private citizens to mine and market them.

We all understand the concept of public and private economies, but think, if you will, of the staggering job of moving a huge country like Russia from one to the other. How would we assign all the houses and apartments in Boston, Winnipeg, and Lubbock to their new private owners? Who would get left out? Who would get too much? Who would get substandard units? What about sons and daughters and cousins and aunts living with families? How would we transfer the hotels, the restaurants, the stores, the shops – how would we place all of these in private hands? Think of the gigantic factories – the result of the sweat, suffering, and sacrifice that produced the Russian industrial revolution: how do we move them to the private sector? Think of the immense wealth that would be up for grabs – in Russia's case, the wealth of one of the world's two superpowers and the natural resources of the world's largest nation. Suddenly all of that wealth would be in play; all of that wealth would need to be moved from a vast government monolithic bureaucracy into the hands of people like you and me. How could it be done?

It never had been done before, and it probably posed the greatest economic and social challenge any modern nation has ever faced. Certainly it was potentially far more disruptive than the herculean task faced by the United States when it mobilized for war in 1941. Transferring this much money from public coffers to private pockets invited corruption and disorder on a scale never before imagined. Violence, cruelty, criminality, dislocation, and political bribery all characterized the United States as it industrialized over

the course of the nineteenth century; try to imagine what life would have
been like in America if the whole shebang of industrialization from the
1890s was picked up wholesale and plopped down in the newly independent
America of 1776. Imagine the United States trying to create a new country
and a new form of government, maintain order in a revolutionary society,
and pick its way internationally among hostile and friendly nations – all while
its citizens embraced a completely new style of life and competed with each
other for economic preferment and massive sums of money.

The Russian mind also had to be privatized. My Moscow friends told me
that the practical aspects of economic change might not have been any
more challenging than the psychological shock administered to the men-
tality of Soviet citizens who were unprepared for all the choices and uncer-
tainties that accompanied a free market. For four generations, most of the
pathways of life had been clearly marked by the central government. Now,
the freedom to be rich, the freedom to take a chance, the freedom to be
daring and different – all these freedoms were dangled in front of an
amazed citizenry, but they came intertwined with the freedom to fail and
starve and not know what to do. Bosses no longer answered to the party but
instead to balance sheets, owners, and stockholders; clerks had to please
customers; barbers had to give stylish haircuts or lose clients. In particular,
the free market's adrenaline shot of hope and fear altered the life cycle.
Students had new opportunities and worries; employees who had expected
to stay at the same job until retirement found themselves looking for new
work as a bloated workforce readjusted to the profit mechanism and the
defense industry contracted; retirees who had expected a dreary but
dependably secure old age now faced penury.

Put simply, Russians not only had to act differently, they had to think
differently: it was as if they emigrated to an entirely new world without
ever having left their home. I believe that every jot of life that I witnessed
in Russia was the result of the people of a country struggling to take the
train of history completely off one track and put it on another. Only if we
try to stretch our minds to comprehend the enormity of the privatization
process can we begin to understand the excesses and extremes of Russian
life in the twenty-first century.

Intimately bound into the privatization process and equally important
to understanding present-day Russia is a simple question with no clear

answer: What should Russians and the world do with Soviet history? Much of the world would simply like to forget it or hold it up as an example of history gone wrong. The West commonly portrays the era from 1917 to 1991 as a blot on humanity that has little redeeming value. Anti-communists blur the Soviet Union with Nazi Germany and blur Stalin with Hitler. Germans have come to terms with their own terrible era in a relatively simple way: they revile it and tend to blame Nazi atrocities substantially on a small group of evil men who hijacked their country. Whether true or not, this intellectual construction works for most Germans today and allows them to face themselves and the world with a minimum of historical schizophrenia and present embarrassment. And, of course, the history of Germany under Nazi rule – as terrible as it was – lasted less than fifteen years.

The Soviet past is far more complicated, and most Russians are unwilling to consign it to the historical scrap heap. The Soviet experiment lasted nearly three-fourths of a century and encompassed four generations of people; it had some extraordinary accomplishments in industrial production, education, science, and social engineering; its aims were utopian; it toppled an oppressive monarchy and destroyed an equally oppressive class structure; and, more than any other country, it sacrificed its citizens to defeat the scourge of fascism. It did all of the above in the face of the implacable opposition of much of the world.

But, of course, ultimately Soviet history failed. The Soviet Union is no more. It wobbled to a death brought on by economic inefficiency, compromised altruism, and yearnings for freedom. Moreover, most Russians fully realize that Soviet accomplishments did sometimes come at a high historical price. Yet, they feel – and they are absolutely right – that the Soviet past must not be conflated with the Nazi past. Russians are not willing – nor should they be – to say that for seventy-five years their great-grandparents, their grandparents, and their parents were either evil villains or naïve dupes.

Historical failure should not require a society either to apologize for the actions of its forebears or to practice historical amnesia and wish its past away. Ironically, the worst excesses of Soviet repression did that to individuals who fell from favor: censors removed their pictures and biographies from encyclopedias. Soviet history requires greater nuance. Russians are struggling now to identify a useable and honest past for themselves,

LIVING WITH STALIN'S GHOST

and they are struggling even more to find ways to bring a balanced sense of Soviet history to their new friends in the rest of the world.

Beyond this large issue of historical cosmology that bedevils Russia at the moment, Soviet history has another and perhaps more immediate effect on the world that people like myself experience when traveling there. Soviet history created a unique set of relations among its citizens – clerks and customers, waiters and diners, faculty and students, bureaucrats and students, the police and the citizenry. After four generations of Soviet history, all of these relationships differed profoundly from the same relationships in the capitalist West, and now people are struggling to find their own identity in the newly capitalistic Russia. It is no easy task.

I titled this memoir *Living with Stalin's Ghost* because Stalin's legacy haunts the new Russia and is shorthand for the Soviet legacy. No one symbolizes the direction and growth of the Soviet Union more than Stalin, no Soviet leader bears more of the weight of the world's contempt, and no Soviet leader is as controversial in present-day Russia. Since 1999, President Vladimir Putin has had the unenviable job of dealing with Stalin's legacy both practically and metaphorically. If President Putin moves too quickly in one direction, he is accused of being a neo-Stalinist; if he delays or hesitates to act in another way, he is accused of being weak and selling his country's history to the highest bidders; if he tries to influence events in the small countries bordering Russia, he is re-imposing Soviet imperialism; if he does not assert Russian interests in its own diplomatic backyard, he is accused of allowing the world led by the United States and Europe to isolate and humiliate Russia and reduce it to small-power status.

The problems faced by President Putin as he deals with the Soviet legacy sound geopolitical in scope, and of course they are, but they bring home an important lesson to us all – the one taught to Ronald Reagan by Tip O'Neill, the genial former Speaker of the U.S. House of Representatives: *All politics is local.* Everything that I observed in Moscow – all the mundane realities of daily life in present Russia – were directly shaped by these large geopolitical issues. If they were not, the issues would not be large – they would not be important. Thus, as this professor taught history at Moscow State University and as this father walked around Moscow, he experienced the most interesting spring of his lifetime as he taught and walked in the shadows of Stalin's past and Putin's present.

Russia is a Hard Country to Know
Do Not Trust First Impressions

I looked more out of place than any other person in Texas as I stood in line to board the plane from Lubbock to Houston. And that is not because I cannot look like a Texan – I can if I want to. But from my Winnipeg days I owned a parka good for arctic weather that I wanted to bring to Russia; if packed it would take up a small suitcase. Carrying it seemed the easiest thing to do, but when also carrying a laptop computer and two briefcases of teaching notes that I did not trust to the airline's baggage destroyers, wearing the parka seemed the only reasonable way to get it on the plane. Thus on a lovely day with temperatures poking into the high 70s, a sweaty American/Canadian wearing a heavy, hooded coat waited in line with a bunch of students wearing t-shirts and left Lubbock, Texas. I would often look just as much out of place during the next six months.

Changing planes in Houston and Amsterdam brought more of the same strange stares: probably only the laptop prevented offers of spare change from kind strangers who thought I was down on my luck. But the wisdom of my decision became apparent when our pilot announced as we approached Moscow that we would be landing in a blizzard. I had been to Moscow's Sheremetyevo airport once before as a tourist in 1993 and had been forced to wait over one hour in line to go through immigration and then another hour to get my luggage. No one had been friendly, no one had been kind, and everyone had shouted bewildering commands in Russian that I had no chance of obeying. By all accounts that I had heard since, the situation had deteriorated even further. The Fulbright office in Washington warns all travelers to expect the worst – so I did. But nothing came close to the worst. I sailed through passport control and customs in fifteen minutes, and my luggage was waiting for me on the other side.

So also was a young guy named Alexey who I had been told would pick me up. Alexey stood holding a sign saying "Fulbright," and I was pretty sure that meant me so I introduced myself. Alexey grabbed a couple of bags, I grabbed a couple, and away we went into what the newspapers would say two days later was Moscow's worst blizzard in four centuries of recorded weather history. In reality, it was not that bad: winds of 30 kph, temperature of $-17\,°C$, and perhaps a total of sixteen inches of snow. Just an average *spring* day in Winnipeg. The fabled brutal Russian winter that everyone seems to think is the worst cold weather in the world is simply not that fierce. If you are Napoleon and are trying to move 100,000 troops from Poland to Moscow, or if you are a German soldier at Stalingrad being resisted by a few million Russian patriots, I am sure that the cold and snow might wear on you a bit. But I lived through what Muscovites say was the worst winter in years and it was roughly comparable to Boston and much better than Northern New England, the Northern Great Plains, and all of Canada except British Columbia. Indeed I believe it is the fabled failed winter military campaigns that have made the west so erroneously think of Russia as frozen tundra.

My first four or five days in Moscow was the only time in my trip that I asked myself a few times if I had made a mistake taking my new job. After this short settling-in process, however, every subsequent week was glorious. During the first few days I kept telling myself that I should not be upset by a few early difficulties. But I was. More than being disheartening, much of what I saw puzzled me. Moscow did not make sense at first and seemed awash in contradiction and paradox. The lesson to be learned from my early thoughts, of course, is that one should never trust first impressions of a new place and people. A combination of natural anxieties, jet lag, and cultural differences made me cranky and clouded my vision.

Back to Alexey and my introduction to Moscow. It took nearly two hours to get to my apartment because of rush-hour traffic and the blizzard conditions, which (despite my above winter commentary) did make driving difficult especially when we got inside the city, which has a poor snow-removal capacity. I certainly had a strong positive first impression about Alexey. He was close to finishing his Ph.D. on the crisis in NATO during the 1960s; he gave me a wonderfully articulate tour of all we passed en route, and he was solicitous of any concerns I had. When I asked Alexey if he would make a career in government or as a professor after finishing his Ph.D., he replied, "I will be a scholar" with such solemnity that I asked him to repeat it to make sure I had heard correctly. When I asked him if he had traveled abroad, he told me he had just arrived back from London two days earlier and had been to New York and Washington in previous years.

I was also grateful for Alexey's welcome because all tourist brochures, western governments, and businesses warn visitors not to take a cab from the Moscow airport. Gypsy cab drivers may rob you and legally licensed ones may extort you for huge sums. So the Fulbright office always hires a driver to pick up anyone coming to Moscow under its auspices. This was the grungiest rented car that I had ever seen, but I was mighty pleased to be in it and not out on some highway emptying my wallet.

We drove through a main square, Smolenskaya, near the apartment I had rented via e-mail on the recommendation of an American who was leaving Moscow. We drove down a dingy street behind the square, a dingier side street, and then a dark alley to a ratty door. This was it. It looked pretty bad, but I know that looks can be deceiving – I am a worldly guy – so I withheld judgment. The driver rang a bell and we were buzzed in to a hallway that made the alley look charming. I withheld judgment no more. A dark staircase that looked like it belonged in an 1890s Brooklyn tenement; cardboard and cigarette butts on the floor; a row of mailboxes several of which hung open; trash discarded everywhere; peeling paint; chunks of materials missing from stairs – it did not look like the entranceway to an $800-a-month apartment.

The building did have an elevator and we took it to my third-floor apartment where my new landlord, Anatoly, was waiting. Anatoly spoke no English but appeared anxious to please, and with Alexey interpreting we got down to brass tacks. I paid him two months rent in American currency (upon which he insisted); he filled out all sorts of complicated papers for my visa registration, which as my landlord he was required to do if he rented to a non-Russian; he showed me the various tricks of the place – how to lock and unlock the two massive locks on the door, how to light the stove, where to put the trash, how to work the washing machine without a permit from the antique bureau, and so on. He was earnest and I was grateful for what appeared to be real kindness.

Here is what one gets in central Moscow – and central is the key word here, since location jacks up all prices massively – for $800 American dollars a month: one room for sleeping, entertaining, eating, and so forth that measures nineteen by eleven feet; a commode in a claustrophobic crevice; a bathroom with tub and basin in which the tub takes up almost all the space; and a kitchen with what appears to be vintage 1930s fridge, stove, and washing machine. For furnishings, four dinner plates, five unmatched glasses, three formerly-Teflon-coated pans, one wine glass, a bed with a thin mattress, a large round table with four wooden chairs, a bureau, two lamps, and a free-standing wooden closet. I will confess to being horrified, but here is where first impressions were wrong.

First, I left out two wonderful features which I did not appreciate that first night. I had a direct view overlooking the Moscow River and illuminating a lovely urban skyline. Under the large windows that spanned the entire room was an inside wooden ledge about two feet wide on which I often sat, sipping wine out of my one glass and contemplating the river and city. It was beautiful and almost assuredly added much to the location variable to boost the rent substantially. The view proved to be a source of great relaxation and poetry for my soul throughout my stay. And, second, the bathtub was so large that I could stretch out completely and still would have had room for a fleet of toy boats in an endless supply of hot water. Who needs three big rooms or modern appliances when one is lucky enough to have a view and a bathtub like that? Forget the horror of opening night – I quickly came to love the apartment; for a person living alone, it was perfect.

As much as I had tried not to bring my North American norms with me, I did not really understand Russian norms at first. Before leaving Texas, I had imagined Russian flats would be like those of England and France that I had seen – smaller than American ones, but well appointed and charming, perhaps even cute. Most of the apartments that I have since seen in Moscow – even those of distinguished professors and professionals – are astonishingly small and spare by American, English or French standards. Russians live in small places because most people have not been able to afford larger places. I bought some dishes and a radio and CD player for my flat and was as happy as a clam there. I also believe that my place was safe despite the dingy entrance.

I met a third person my first night: Professor Yuri Rogulev, my designated contact person at the university, who entered the apartment with a bag of groceries for me about ten minutes after I arrived. Yuri proved to be as nice as Alexey and Anatoly, both of whom were deferential to him; I could tell that he was regarded as a person of consequence. I knew that he had authored at least two books on American labor history, had once been a Fulbright senior scholar in the other direction, and had taught labor history in the United States. After unpacking the groceries, all four of us went out into the night—Alexey and Anatoly back to their own homes while Yuri walked me to Smolenskaya, a large square surrounded by retail businesses, to show me several stores where I could shop for food. The square seemed nearly deserted at about 7:30 p.m.—I learned later that this was only because of the storm—but both stores we went in were full of shoppers.

Yuri walked me back home, wished me well, and at 8 p.m., having not slept in more than twenty-four hours, I was on my own in Moscow.

LESS CHARMING IMPRESSIONS

Friday morning I trundled around Smolenskaya buying stuff. I wanted maps of the metro and city and an English newspaper, the *Herald Tribune,* which is sold all over Europe. News kiosks are everywhere and I must have gone to twenty of them asking for the *Tribune.* Uniformly, the proprietors—both men and women—scowled, turned away, and offered no help; it was as if I was wearing a "kick me" sign. I finally got the paper only after seeing it in a kiosk window and pointing at it. The *Tribune* lists what it should cost in each country, and the price for Russia was high—$4 US. The clerk charged me 170 rubles, however, which turned out to be about $7 US. This proved to be one of the cheapest *Tribunes* I would buy during my stay. The price has gone as high as $8 and all the pointing in the world at the $4 sign did not help one bit. The price was what the clerk said.

And so it went with virtually every clerk in every store: they all seemed unhelpful, impatient, and rude—not just to me but to everyone. They all took the same two-year course that required sullen stares and allowed no smiles or else you did not graduate. Life on the street seemed pretty much the same. No one held a door for anyone going in or out of a building or metro stop, no one murmured "excuse me" if they bumped into someone, no one passed the time of day with strangers at a corner by saying "some weather." It was as if everyone I met was having the worst day of his or her life – but having it every day. I found this perplexing and unsettling. The truth was, though, that it seemed to me in those first few days that all Russians – with the exceptions of Alexey, Anatoly, and Yuri – were grumpy.

MY COLLEAGUES

Shopping for food proved equally horrifying – at first – but it also gave me a possible explanation for everyone's bad mood. I did my early shopping in the two stores that Yuri had taken me to and although I knew in advance of the trip that Moscow was the third most expensive city in the world in which to live, I was unprepared for these prices. Unattractive oranges, $2 each; potatoes, more than $1 each; grapes about $14 per pound; small flats of blueberries about $14; a jar of peanut butter, $5. Fish was the worst: Cod was $28 a pound and it looked as if it did not smell good.

What was cheap? Cheeses were everywhere and looked good and were just slightly higher than in Texas or Manitoba. Eggs were about $1.50 a dozen, a relative bargain. Sausages and salamis looked really good and were about the same price as in the U.S. and Canada. Cigarettes – including American brands such as Marlboro – were about a dollar a pack. Every store and kiosk sold beer and vodka and other booze, and it was incredibly cheap.

I concocted two early theories of life in Moscow based on public behavior, supply, demand, and pricing.

THEORY ONE. All of Moscow was constipated because no one could afford to buy anything that had fiber in it and everyone was forced to live on cheeses and sausages that plugged one up: this explained the ubiquitous unfriendly behavior. A few tons of strategically placed celery stalks could work miraculous personality transformations, I thought. On that first day of shopping, I imagined a possible conversation in a new fiber-rich world:

"How are you, Mr. Daniels? So nice to see you in my shop. Thanks for the celery. It is just what a shopkeeper needs to stay happy. Oops, got to go for a minute. Be right back. Make yourself at home."

THEORY TWO. Muscovites acted crabby because everything that was healthy was too expensive and everything that was unhealthy was cheap. For good reason, this would put many people in a bad mood, and it would also explain the massive amount of public drinking and inebriation revealed by even a cursory walk around Moscow. People drank a lot because they knew Theory Two and it was depressing.

At the end of my trip, I still stand behind my observations about the inadequacy of public civility, but I no longer attribute it to inherent nasty dispositions or depression over unhealthy food or constipation – although I do think the latter must be a problem considering the diet. And I would completely refine my description of the behavior and substitute a new explanation for it. The principle that governs public intercourse is that of complete non-involvement with strangers. Do not interact with people whom you do not know and, if you must – as in a customer-clerk relationship – keep the interaction minimal.

There are historic and cultural reasons for such a strident philosophy of active non-engagement. The main proposition is that one should mind one's own business; no one ever got in trouble by keeping his mouth shut. Secondarily, by everyone's account, the Soviet era provided few incentives for clerks and wait staff to go out of their way to please customers. It may also be that we in the West are too accustomed to thinking that service people have a duty to make their customers happy.

Moreover, to some degree this standoffish behavior characterizes big cities everywhere, and I am certain that small-town Russia could not possibly hold as many citizens as Moscow does who go through life with this stare-straight-ahead, don't-make-eye-contact attitude. And, of course, Americans are infamously garrulous, often to the annoyance of those who don't want to make a new friend on the train or plane. But the coldness I experienced on my early outings around Smolenskaya exceeded urban/rural or American/European contrasts. I did not feel comfortable with it.

Those first few days, however, I did not observe closely enough the behavior of Muscovites with their friends and family. To counterbalance the negative impressions of the street and shop, all one has to do is go into any Russian home or social environment. I subsequently became overwhelmed with the kindness, generosity, and warmth of virtually everyone I met. Moscow is a city of huggers and kissers as soon as one passes through a private door. It is *bizarre:* the personal character is the complete opposite of the public one. Friends and lovers in cafés and restaurants are cheerful and animated and expressive towards each other. Russian girls and women almost always link arms as they walk together, which is also true of women throughout much of Europe and always looks sweet to me. The girls kiss each other on the cheeks in the French mode when they meet, and this is equally endearing. The boys all shake hands with each other every single morning when they meet at the university. People bring little gifts to each other for the smallest of occasions. People give each other flowers so much that it seems as if every third person walking down the street has a bouquet tucked under the arm. Muscovites are cold and unresponsive to people they do not know but are wonderful to those that they do.

Very quickly, I had to refine my thoughts on pricing also and my early negative impression faded – but not entirely – when I learned to live and shop as Muscovites did. By all official accounts, Moscow is indeed dreadfully expensive, but almost every price that I saw in the first few days was halved if I shopped outside of one of those two big supermarkets and went to one of the dozens of little grocery stores that dot every neighborhood. And outdoor markets were even cheaper. One near the university had reasonable quality bananas, plums, and oranges for just a little more than I would pay in Texas. At its cheapest, meat is at least twice as much as in the United States or Canada, and fish even more highly priced and of general overall lower quality. But the shock from those first impressions at the two major grocery stores quickly wore off because those prices were so inordinately out of line with daily reality. Strangely enough, American and Canadian small Mom and Pop groceries usually charge more than the big stores; in Moscow small stores charge much less.

On my salary Moscow was quite livable, but for my colleagues at the University who make between $120 and $500 a month or for most Muscovites, who make far less, it remains a mystery to me how they survive as well as they do. Most of them, however, say they almost never shop in central Moscow because the prices are outrageous even in the smaller stores: thus, my new cheaper prices – half of the big markets – could be lessened significantly more if I had the time, patience, and know-how to venture out to remote markets. It is in downtown Moscow only, not all of Russia or even the greater Moscow area, that food is so prohibitively expensive, but everyone I met did complain that no matter where in the country one bought food, prices were dramatically higher than two or three years ago.

As the disquietude of those first few days began to be replaced by much more enjoyable experiences, I realized that Moscow and Russia required more thought and work than many places I had been, and that this was nearly as true for Muscovites as it was for me. Survival and knowledge here were hard won, and everything was not always what it seemed to be on the surface. I have tried to keep my own introduction in mind as I introduce my experiences in the following chapters.

CHAPTER ONE

Life at Moscow State University
Russia's Greatest University at Risk

Before seeing Moscow State University, my home for the semester, I had a chance to learn about it from two sources, both of which left me with an extraordinarily positive impression of what I was likely to experience once I began teaching. I had dinner at the home of the department chair, Professor Eugene Yazkov, and I toured the Kremlin with a young student, Irina Kovaleva, who was enrolled in my class. I will never forget either occasion.

DINNER AT THE YAZKOVS'

Professor Eugene Yazkov is the Chair of Modern and Contemporary History, one of the six subdivisions of the Department of History. The entire department, including Medieval, Ancient, and Russian, has more than two hundred members; the Modern and Contemporary section has more than fifty members. On my second night in Moscow, Professor Yazkov invited me to dinner on the next Saturday afternoon, and there I had my first formal meal in a Russian house.

You could travel around the world twice and never meet as accomplished, attractive, enjoyable, and kind a couple as Eugene and Marina Yazkov. Professor Yazkov was 83 years old when I met him. He has authored several books on American farmer protests, teaches a full course load, administers a large department, and still supervises theses. Corridor rumor thinks Marina is a year or two older than her husband.

The much-put-upon Alexey was assigned to pick me up and get me to the Yazkovs; I think he was quite pleased to get a chance to have a meal at the house of this renowned couple. Getting there without Alexey would have required three different metros, which I could have done, but then picking my way around dozens of large apartment complexes on the outskirts of Moscow probably would have exceeded my capability. The area seemed surprisingly forested and village-like despite the fact that probably at least ten thousand people lived in these complexes. Alexey called Marina several times to home in on the right block.

When we arrived, Professor Yazkov gave me a quick up and down look and then said, "Welcome, my friend, we are so glad you are here," followed by a hug – we are talking the old Brezhnev bear hug, not some puny embrace – followed by real kisses on each cheek. Then he stood back and introduced Marina and she did the same. It was so unexpectedly affectionate and sweet. Then they both hugged and kissed Alexey and then they introduced me to a young man, Sasha, who turned out to be one of the most intense and bright graduate students I have ever met.

I, in turn, surveyed the Yazkovs. The professor is about 5'8", 130 pounds, looks remarkably fit, has startling blue eyes and a full head of white hair, and was absolutely bubbling with life. Marina is tiny, about 5'2" and 110 pounds, and one of the most beautiful women I have ever seen. The two could be models for a perfect older couple anywhere in the world.

But there was much more. After some pleasantries, Professor Yazkov ushered us all into his office to show me in particular, but also Alexey and Sasha, a rogue's gallery of pictures of all my predecessors in the Sivachev Chair. He was immensely proud of the program, and I already knew that to a great extent he was responsible for its lasting and thriving under political circumstances that were often difficult. The Fulbright Program in general, and the Sivachev Chair most particularly, were shining beacons of intellectual light and friendship in the darkest, most frigid years of the Cold War.

In the office, I noticed two pictures of Marina as a very young woman that could not be more different. In one she is posed with a cello; in the other, an army uniform. Not surprisingly, this refined woman made her living and had a career as a professional cellist. After being prevailed upon by the other three men, Marina brought out a box of medals from World War II. This tiny cellist fought in and survived the Battle of Stalingrad, one of the bloodiest battles in human history. Later in the war she received serious wounds fighting in Ukraine. For her exceptional bravery, she received a chestful of glorious colored medals of which she was deservedly proud.

Several more hugs were exchanged during all of this, and both Yazkovs asked me questions about my family and seemed very pleased that I was a grandfather. Then we went into the dining room precisely at 2 p.m. to start dinner. *What a dinner.* Marina had somehow sneaked out and piled a lot of food on the table. We all took our places and Professor Yazkov opened a bottle of vodka and poured some in everyone's glass and then made an elegant toast to their "distinguished guest" (that was me, in case you wouldn't know). After we had been eating about five minutes, Professor Yazkov made a second toast to the wonderful cook of all the food — Marina — and told me proudly that she made everything by hand with no prefabricated ingredients. The next toast was to my three daughters and my grandson — how did he remember so precisely? I forget the subject of most of the next few, but there were many. I did notice, however, that everyone was discreet; this was not a drunken lunch. When dinner was finally over nearly three hours later, and with five of us drinking to each toast, the bottle of vodka still had a sliver of liquid.

What a life the Yazkovs have led, and how much of Russia's twentieth-century history has been joined with their own! They both lament — but not at great length, and with more sadness than bitterness — their perception that the new consumer-capitalist generation does not appreciate the sacrifices made by generations of Soviet people to make Russia an industrialized power and to win the war against the fascists. Despite their great station at the university, the Yazkovs live in what appeared to be a simple three-room apartment with kitchen and bath in a dilapidated old building. And they could not seem happier. Professor Yazkov has traveled to the United States several times for research and to teach, but a few years ago he and Marina traveled together and visited as honored guests at the campuses of more than a dozen of the holders of the Sivachev Chair. For obvious reasons, the two are revered, and I place myself in their legions of admirers.

For the three years before I came to Moscow, I had been chair of the department of history at Texas Tech University, so Professor Yazkov and I engaged in some chair-talk at dinner. He of course had vastly more experience, having been chair of the Modern section since 1980, when his predecessor had died in office. Professor Yazkov showed no signs that he was contemplating retiring either from teaching or administration, and my guess is that he will end his tenure in the chair in the same manner as his predecessor – when he is no longer able to sit upright. I was curious how a chair functioned at this great university and asked him some direct questions. Moscow State's press publishes many books in history; who decides what is and is not published? "It is my decision," Professor Yazkov said simply. Who decides about hiring? The same answer: "It is my decision." Are there committees formed to help you hire? "I ask the opinions of others, sometimes," Professor Yazkov replied.

None of the above was said with any pomp or puffery; it was merely stated as fact. Department chairs in Russia are essentially appointed to be bosses of their department, as opposed to North America, where they are appointed to mediate among contending factions, receive the reports of various committees that are mandated to perform specific functions, and represent the department to the higher levels of administration. I do not know of a modern-day chair in North America who could or would make the same simple declarations that Professor Yazkov made in such a matter-of-fact manner. The difference between Russian and North American chairs is extraordinary.

Possessing such authority, however, did not make Professor Yazkov authoritarian in manner. Sasha and Alexey clearly held Professor Yazkov in great esteem; he in turn was affectionate and easygoing with them. All three discussed Russian politics with equal energy, and all three helped Marina Yazkov clear the table but insisted that I remain sitting. Moreover, Professor Yazkov knew the names and backgrounds of many of the students that I would have in my class.

At many truly great universities, individual students get lost in the academic shuffle of what the great scholars believe to be more important matters, but I sensed already that this was not the case at Moscow State. Before the week was over, I would meet my first undergraduate student who would more than confirm the impressions I formed at the Yazkovs.

MY FIRST MAJOR OUTING TO MUSEUMS

Quite extraordinarily to my sensibilities – it would not be likely to happen in North America – each of the students in my class is more or less assigned to take me on an outing each weekend. The rationale, I believe, is that it helps students get to know the Sivachev Chair as a potential contact for further study in America, as well as polishing their English skills. I am sure that if a student refuses, no punishment would be forthcoming, but I do not think many decline, and I have a hunch they like the opportunity. For the visiting Fulbrighters, it is a good deal because they get a knowledgeable guide and an informal opportunity to learn a lot about Russia, and Russian education in particular.

The guide for my first outing before classes started was Irina Kovaleva, a young woman of twenty-two who has just finished the Russian equivalent of a master's thesis, a 140-page analysis of the precursors to women's reform in the second quarter of the nineteenth century–Jacksonian America. Quite simply, she seems brilliant, accomplished, and poised beyond almost all twenty-two-year-olds that I have met; she is completely trilingual in Russian, English, and Spanish; she is profoundly proud of her country's history and culture even though she wishes to continue in American history for her Ph.D. She has strong and clear opinions, which she expresses politely, but also confesses to being an "old-fashioned girl." I quote her precise words because her definition of "old-fashioned girl" would confound our sense of the term in some ways. But as we will see, it makes great sense upon a little reflection.

Irina phoned me the day before our outing and asked what I would like to see. I suggested the Kremlin, and she immediately agreed. We met at her suggestion in a metro station. Irina wore a beautiful suede coat, a stylish fur hat, had a very chic hair style and glasses, and was clearly quite attentive to her appearance, although I mean to suggest no shallowness on her part; far from it. I mention this not out of sexism but because her appearance is important to her definition of "old-fashioned." She first used that term later in the day in response to my question as to whether young Russian men and women lived together before they were married. Some did, she allowed, but not many, and certainly not as many as in the Western world. She herself thought cohabitation before marriage was wrong.

An only child, Irina obviously has two self-sacrificing parents who adore her and are immensely proud of her scholarly accomplishments. She was devoting herself to American women's history and, indeed, to studying radical movements in women's history. She clearly believed that the United States had leagues to go before women would have a fair shake in society–although she loved the fact that American men cooked, and lamented the fact that almost no Russian men did. "Old-fashioned" Irina clearly was a feminist and looked forward to more progress in the United States, which she regarded as lagging somewhat behind in the feminist march, despite the fact that men did some of the cooking. She also looked back in most ways to an idyllic version of her own country that lay in the Soviet past. When I asked Irina about the meaning of the new Russian flag, she replied with disdain that it had no meaning at all and was just a gaudy symbol of the present nothingness.

At some point in the afternoon, a light flashed on in my head: Being an "old-fashioned girl" for Irina meant looking back to the best of the Soviet past—she was a Communist. By this I do not mean that Irina was an activist today, or a Communist Party member, but simply that she was immensely proud of many of the accomplishments of the Soviet era and believed that she was currently living in a time of regression and self-indulgence that betrayed many of the great strides forward made by the generations since the Russian Revolution. Upon any small amount of reflection, much about the Soviet world would appeal to the feminist in Irina; probably no area on earth brought women more professional, educational and financial equality than the Soviet governments. The Soviet era also asserted Russia's role as one of the world's two dominant superpowers, and of course that appealed to Irina, the old-fashioned patriot. And finally, in the Soviet era, governments and society emphasized a clean, clear morality—no prostitution, no street crime, no western decadence such as boys and girls living together out of wedlock. Ironically, the Soviet governments, which disdained religion, created a social universe much more closely patterned on basic Christian morals than did the Christian-dominated Western world in the same era.

In one of the several museums to which Irina took me, she showed me a wonderful series of Soviet-era posters from the 1930s and 1950s that bracketed the war years. These posters would remind almost any American of Norman Rockwell's *Saturday Evening Post* covers—clean-cut paeans to family values and virtues. The posters showed sweet, sincere, wholesome, smiling, healthy young boys and girls pursuing education, helping others, sacrificing gladly for the good of their community and nation—the posters showed, of course, Irina's parents and their generation at their ideal best.

After being together for about four hours, during which we were bonded somewhat by genuinely freezing winds on our walkabout in the

Kremlin, I began to feel very paternal towards Irina, and for reasons you will see below, my admiration grew by leaps and bounds. At a coffee house after our long afternoon, I asked her what her parents did for a living – I assumed that they both worked outside the house – and she told me that her mother was a licensed engineer and her father a computer technologist. When I expressed the opinion that they must do well, she shook her head vigorously and said that following *perestroika* and the Gorbachev reforms, both her parents lost their jobs in state-owned companies and had been unable to replace them with comparable ones. More reasons, of course, for Irina to look back with fondness to "old-fashioned" times.

The tour of the Kremlin proved remarkable for three reasons: (1) the Kremlin is stunning, particularly the plaza of the three great cathedrals; (2) the degree of difficulty we had in seeing things because of the petty tyrants who masquerade as guards; and (3) the amount of knowledge Irina had about all that we saw. I wish to tell about the difficulties and of Irina and not about the Kremlin itself because I think my own experience there is more interesting and instructive.

Visitors must buy tickets to walk on the Kremlin grounds, although Irina told me that fifteen years ago, Russians and foreigners alike could freely stroll about without notice or cost. She and her friends often played there. I lamented this as a sad fact of recent life and said that, alas, the self-guided tours of the White House had ended after the events of 9/11 and would likely never be resumed. Irina replied that she believed that money more than security lay behind the Kremlin's controlled access. Irina was a cheap date because, wonderfully enough, university students are so esteemed in Russia that their student cards get them into most historic sites and museums for free. Pity the poor kid, however, who is selling CDs in a little kiosk at half the average salary and would like to see a bit of his or her history. Even though Russian nationals pay about one-fifth of the amount charged foreigners for admission, the ticket price still would be burdensome.

Most foreigners require tour guides, but I do not because I have Irina. After we wait in line, however, for fifteen long, cold minutes, Irina and the ticket seller have a long and contentious conversation. The woman was rude and dismissive and, as far as I could tell, without any cause. Wrong line, as it turned out. The booth we were in sold tickets only to guided tours. What to do? Irina got directions to the right booth, which turned out to be two or three hundred yards down the wall. We follow a stream of other people who made the same mistake; nothing on the sign indicated that the first line was for people on tours only. So we repeat the wait, and once again the exchange between Irina and this ticket-master seems equally difficult. As we waited in line, I tried to observe other ticket purchases, and always the conversation seemed scratchy. I ponied up some more money for a tour of the Armory, as the main Kremlin museum is called, and Irina informed me that the museum visit was causing the problem, not the visit to the Kremlin grounds themselves. One had to set an exact time for entrance to the Armory, and if one was late, there was no admittance. You snooze, you lose.

Finally, we were on the beautiful grounds. I was about to say that visitors were surprisingly few in number – but considering the weather, the cost, the confusion, and the snarky ticket sellers, perhaps the place was overflowing. Most of the buildings are off limits because the Kremlin is still the seat of government; presumably high-level decision-making is going on within a stone's throw of where we strolled. As we walked and Irina talked, I was amazed by her detailed knowledge of all the major buildings. Without fail, she knew their construction dates, architects, problems, artistic strengths and weaknesses, folklore, famous incidents, and everything else imaginable.

Whew. Remember, Irina did not suggest that we visit the Kremlin, I did. It is not her specialty. Nor is she an art historian or even a Russian historian: She is a historian of American women's movements. I have spent my adult life writing about New England's colonial capitals, but I could not begin to give one-quarter of the tour of Boston, Hartford, or Providence that Irina could of the Kremlin. And she positively brimmed with pride. Irina did not just look back fondly to the golden era of Soviet worldly accomplishment; she welled up with love for Russian culture over the past millennium, and she clearly felt a great joy in sharing this culture with me.

The inside guards – brusque, rude clones of the outside ticket sellers – provided the only irritant to this deeply moving experience. If I were with a tour of foreigners, I would have assumed that the hostility was directed personally against tourists, and it would be a little more understandable; but Irina was as polite and as Russian as anyone could be. I wondered then, and still do now, if perhaps these guards do not like students.

So, that was my first student outing and it was a dandy. The next time someone portrays Soviet Russia as nothing but an evil empire of thick, oppressive brutes, I would like you to think of the brilliant, cultivated, trilingual, feminist, feminine, sweet, kind, patriotic Irina. An "old-fashioned girl."

As a little addendum to the above, I would not wish to suggest that Irina and others are not aware of the dark side of the Soviet era; nor are they immune to enjoying many of the pleasures and improvements of the new capitalist era. I do mean to suggest, however, that the one-dimensional pictures that historic enemies paint of each other do a dreadful injustice to the complex ways in which men and women struggle to live in the best of all possible worlds.

MY FIRST DAY ON THE JOB

Having been introduced to the faculty and students of Moscow State on two wonderful social occasions, it now was time for me to earn my keep and be introduced to the classroom. Despite having been in this business a long time, I was nervous. For one thing, many of my predecessors in the Sivachev Chair had been genuine luminaries – icons in the world of historians – and I was anxious not to fall short of their high standards. Second, although the class has only twenty students, usually many of the senior American historians on the faculty attend; they are all smart, and I assume they are quite willing to be critical. So I prepared carefully for my first lecture and tossed and turned in bed a bit the night before.

A few words about Moscow State University. By leaps and bounds it is the oldest, largest, and most prestigious school in all of Russia. It is more than Russia's Harvard because there is no Yale or Princeton nipping at its heels. It may well be the preeminent university on the entire Eurasian landmass, because its professors write most of the textbooks that are used for all subjects in most other Russian universities and in many of the universities in the fourteen former Soviet Republics. Almost every American historian I have met or heard of from Moscow State has been a Fulbright Scholar at a prestigious American school. So the joint is a big deal, and by far the best school in which I have ever taught.

Moscow State is celebrating its 250th anniversary this year and has been frequently visited by all Russian leaders for its many occasions and celebrations. The main building of the university – the building that is used as the university's emblem – is one of the spectacular seven sister gothic skyscrapers built by Stalin's orders between 1946 and 1954. The building – the international face of Moscow State – is on the highest hill in the city and is truly breathtaking; but aside from this postcard structure, every other part of this immensely influential institution is a dump. The history department has its own building, but it looks like one of those nightmare public-housing apartment blocks in Chicago that were recently torn down. Every part of it is dirty; the drapes are torn and hanging off the hooks; the stairways are decrepit; the student desks are rickety; many windows and doors are stuck open or ajar: it looks much like my apartment house entrance – grunge everywhere. Professors have no offices; only chairs of the departments do. Professors are not supplied with paper; chalk must be brought to one's own lecture, copying must be paid for personally, and there are no secretarial services. This is the best school in a huge chunk of the world and one of a handful of the most influential universities in the world, and it does not have the faculty and student amenities you would find in any inner-city American high school. It does not have soap in the bathrooms or toilet paper in the stalls, which are simply filthy. All the commodes are missing their seats.

One enters history through two rows of six doors each, but for security reasons only one door in each six-door bank is open. Thus, there is usually a crowd of people trying to go through one door while the other five remain locked; once you are through the first bank, you repeat the problem and delay again in a second queue. After entering the foyer through this annoying procedure, you must go through a metal detector and then present your identification papers to two security guards.

After going through all of this, the first lecture was anticlimactic. My friend from the first night, Yuri Rogulev, introduced me quite graciously to the class and audience and the assemblage clapped loudly after his introduction. The Fulbright Lecture, as these weekly lectures are called, has been scheduled at the same time – 12:10 to 1:30 p.m. – for every year of the Sivachev Chair, so that everyone knows of it and anyone who wants may attend because no other classes are held at the same time. In this case, I counted fifty people. Twenty were my students and I would meet with them in three one-hour seminars each week, one each for the third, fourth, and fifth-year students – "consultations," they are called here. Nine appeared to be faculty, and the others were students who were not enrolled in my class. As I learned after class, at least ten of them were from an English-language class and were assigned to come to take notes on what I said so that they could be quizzed on their English comprehension. The students looked attentive and I tried my best to be entertaining, but could not get a big laugh out of anyone. I later learned that Russian students tend to be more formal and expect more formality in class than Americans or Canadians do.

CONSULTATIONS

During my thirteen weeks of classes, I came to know many students very well, and all of them to some degree. Were I teaching them at the University of Winnipeg or at Texas Tech, I would refer to my students as women and men, but here they call themselves girls and boys. When I inquired about it, they all said that they preferred that–so girls and boys it is. I asked my students to help me learn about Moscow, Russia, and education in this part of the world, and they obliged remarkably. They seemed extremely interested in sharing details of their own individual and collective lives with me–much more so than my North American students, although I realize that this was partially a function of my outsider status.

Before giving you a sample of their opinions and description of their behavior, let me discuss their position and demography.

POSITION. About one-third of Russian students go to university or college, which is probably a European average although far below the 55 percent that currently do so in North America. Near the end of high school, students take exams that to a substantial degree determine whether they may go to university or not. Until the last year or two, tuition was completely free at universities, and it still is for most students who are good enough to be admitted under the high admissions standards of most universities. Moscow State and other schools, however, have started admitting some students who fall a little short on the entrance exams. These students pay for the privilege; thus a two-tiered system is being created.

Ominously (from my point of view) the government has announced that it wishes to change this and begin charging all students some tuition. Such a policy would change the very nature of Russian universities, all of

which had been public in the Communist era and continued to be public
for the first decade after the end of the Soviet Union. In addition to
tuition charges at some public schools, some private colleges and universities are opening their doors, and although much less prestigious than the
public ones, they will hasten the process of privatizing this great public system of higher education. The new developments may also lessen the
esteem in which university students (and professors) are held. The term
"student" has more cachet and status in all of Europe than in North America, and Russia is no exception: being a student elicits genuine respect.
Students usually get admitted free to all museums and art galleries or pay
a very nominal fee.

The most prestigious university in the country, Moscow State administers its own admission exam, as do all of the other high-quality schools
such as Saint-Petersburg State University. Some of my students stayed out
of school for a year to study for Moscow's admission exam, which everyone from faculty to students agree is very hard, so getting admitted to
Moscow State is a big deal for a student. It sounds to me much like getting
admitted to Harvard or Yale, except that most of these students do come
from the Moscow area instead of nationwide.

THE DEMOGRAPHICS. I find it fascinating that fifteen of my twenty students are the only child of their families, and each of the other five has
only one sibling. The students all explain these strange data the same way:
having children is expensive, and educating them well is even more
expensive. Thus, most of their parents put all their eggs – or their one egg,
in three-quarters of the cases – in one basket. In one sense, these kids are
spoiled because of all the attention they have received growing up, but in
another sense, being the only child imposes a real responsibility on them
to do well. Most said that they did three or four hours homework every
day during high school and do more now as Moscow State students. Not
surprisingly, my students seemed genuinely surprised to learn that I had
three daughters, which must seem to them to be a big, sprawling bunch.

By definition, all of my students are perfectly bilingual in Russian and
English, but they must be trilingual in order to graduate. Most speak and
write French, German, or Spanish, and several know Italian. One is fluent
in Chinese; when I inquired if she had a special reason for learning Chi-

nese, she said simply that she was interested in it. Another has learned Hungarian. And these kids are not bragging. If they confess to knowing a language, they do, indeed, know it. The criterion for graduation is not merely to pass a test in the language; genuine fluency is required. Most say that they do not know Ukrainian but when pressed will say that they could read a Ukrainian newspaper or understand it if spoken slowly because Slavic languages are similar. In addition to the above language skills, all of my students have taken at least three years of Latin and read it easily.

If fathering a huge brood of three kids shocked my students, my confession of being monolingual positively staggered them. I told them the truth: I had to pass exams in Hindi and French to get a Ph.D., but that I could not speak either beyond the most basic of expressions. They undoubtedly thought they were being taught by an ignoramus – *and they were right.* I may have regained a little stature by telling them that my three daughters – the new generation of Canadians – are bilingual.

Of my twenty students, all have traveled outside of Russia to countries that were once part of the Soviet Union, and sixteen have traveled to countries outside of the old Soviet empire. About half have been to France and England, and seven have been to the United States. Several have been to Italy and Spain, and at least five of them have been to six or seven countries on separate trips. Exotic destinations show up among these trips: China, Africa, Australia, and Japan. One of the four students who have not traveled outside of the former Soviet world gave a strange (at least to me, but not to her fellow students) reason for not having ventured further. Her parents are high-level researchers in the Russian space program and as such cannot get a passport to travel; their disqualifying status at present extends to her. She has applied for a passport twice and been turned down. I found this stunning, but the other students did not.

I pressed my three seminars to make me aware of their thoughts on the future of their country and their own futures. I suggested that they lean back, close their eyes, and imagine what is most likely to transpire in Russia over the next fifteen years. They were shockingly pessimistic. Every student said that the country will get much worse before it gets better, and every one expected a great deal of instability. Many predicted some sort of civil war; all predicted various coups and regional rebellions. Among major problems they cited were the criminal elements who they said control almost all the privatized industries; the crumbling technological infrastructure that had been built by the Soviet but was not being maintained and repaired; dreadful environmental circumstances that were steadily worsening – especially the water supply in cities, which is becoming increasingly unsafe to drink; the impossibility of building a strong economy when the country relies so extensively on the exportation of natural resources; and a government that serves itself, not the people who elected it. These kids were sweet, bright, and getting the best education in the country, and they were cynical beyond any group of students that I have ever encountered.

They also were convinced that historically and at present, the rest of Europe and the United States have been hostile to Russia and have tried to isolate it from the world. No one in eastern or western Europe understands Russia, they all said. From World War I through the Revolution and the 1920s, through World War II and the Cold War, all of the rest of the industrialized world feared Russia and tried to intervene in its internal affairs. Remember please that these students are all doing M.A. theses in American history and are probably more kindly disposed towards the United States than are any other Russians. They see NATO and the European Union incorporating the countries of eastern Europe and the Baltic states into anti-Russian alliances, and it makes them angry – in a remarkably polite, courteous way. When I asked these students if Russia could ever possibly join the European Union, they all said that would be a complete impossibility, for although Moscow is a European city, Russia is more of an Asian country, and it must cast its future with the Central Asian republics that were once part of the Soviet Union.

On their own futures, none of the students had a strong sense of what his or her career would be. Several said that they would like to be professors but could not afford to unless university salaries increased. Most said that their parents had already selected careers when they had been at a similar age and now worried greatly about their children. Only one student said that he would like to emigrate, but several said that they might be forced to, and considered this a bitter but realistic possibility. Once again, I was struck by the depressing futures that these wonderfully sweet kids saw unfolding before themselves.

Near the end of the term, I assigned them to read an essay on the movie versions of Nathaniel Hawthorne's classic novel, *The Scarlet Letter.* It produced a curious discussion that took an unexpected turn. A sentence in the essay stated that understanding *The Scarlet Letter* helped one understand the soul of Puritan New England. One of the students said that he had never read a historian previously who had referred to the American soul but that Russian historians and social commentators often refer to the Russian soul. Every student jumped in on this discussion and it became clear that every one of them believed that Russians had an unusual soul that coursed through all their literature, music, art, and history. Further, they all said that outsiders who made movies or operas or conducted symphonies of Russian content, never could capture the Russian soul and hence always made inartistic, soulless products.

I asked them if I could understand the Russian soul, and they all looked embarrassed but essentially agreed that it was not possible. So I asked them to give me single words to describe the elusive soul. Here are the words they came up with: dark, gloomy, despairing, fatalistic, pessimistic, unhappy, tragic, melancholy, and introverted. When I suggested that these all seemed to be versions of the same theme and it sounded horribly depressing, they agreed but stuck to their guns. "Russians do not expect life to be happy," one said, "and we know there is nothing we can do about it." When I suggested that maybe Russians should get a new soul, they replied with the obvious – that it was impossible. A soul is a soul, and a person or country is stuck with the only one available.

And now came another surprise, but one that upon reflection made a great deal of sense out of other parts of my experience. A student said that Russians would not want a happy new soul because they were extremely patriotic about being Russian and would not want to change. It is clear, however, that patriotism means profoundly different things to Americans and Russians. As Americans, we often start our definition of patriotism by talking about political matters or governance. We are proud of the American Revolution, democracy, the Constitution, the Bill of Rights, fair court trials, an uninterrupted (or nearly so) record of stability for over two centuries, and so forth. My Russian students have no pride in their present government or in any government or governing system of the past. For them, patriotism means a love of Russian culture – a culture that transcends and survives political systems but, unlike American culture, is not based on political systems.

As these students talked about this kind of patriotism I realized how tightly connected to their past these Russian kids felt. One of the strange things about having Russia explained to me by colleagues and students on our various outings is that they laced their explanations with a constant stream of proverbs. We all know how people do this: "there is an old Texas saying ..." or "there is an old New England proverb ..." But in the United States usually proverbial remarks are sparing and particularly associated with old codgers and codgerettes. Not so over here. An average three-hour outing with two twenty-year-old Russian hip students would be peppered with at least ten Russian proverbs. Russian culture reminds me in some ways of a village culture that is grounded on a shared experience that one generation passes on to the next by a sort of cultural osmosis that makes it largely unknowable to outsiders. Despite the size of Russia, it is an insular place with an insular culture – or soul, to use the proper word.

Curiously, the insularity is borne out by the only part of Russian patriotism that has a political definition – resistance to outside attempts to subordinate Russia. And here, the definition is literal. My students, as do all Russians, refer to three great wars in the last two centuries by the following names. The war in which Russia repelled Napoleon's invasion is "The First Patriotic War," World War I is "The Great War," and World War II is "The Great Patriotic War." In the more distant past, Russians commemorate the defeat of the invading Swedish and of the invading Tartars. Russians have a sense that other countries historically always seem to want to conquer Russia. I believe that to a great extent, this sense of being constantly under attack explains the government and public's present response to the expansion of NATO and the European Union throughout eastern Europe, to the interference – perceived or real – of the West in the elections in the countries of the old Soviet Union, and to the West's persistent criticism of the pace of Russia's march to democracy.

On the day of my last lecture to all my students assembled together, I felt a bit nostalgic and sad, as I often did at Winnipeg and Texas Tech, but was unprepared for the way in which the students said goodbye to their professors on what they call in English "The Last Bell." One of my fifth-year students stood up and asked to say a few words and then proceeded to thank me for traveling all this distance to educate them in such a stimulating manner. She then called for another student to stand up and the second one presented me with a lovely bouquet of flowers. I was, needless to say, darn close to tears. As I later found out, I had no need to feel flattered; students do this for all professors, whether or not they like them. It is a lovely tradition that I would like to commend to the West. At the end of one of my consultations, however, I received another present from the class – a bottle of Jack Daniels whiskey which had been cleverly re-lettered to read "Bruce Daniels." This was more of a sign of genuine esteem and, as I thanked the little group, I realized that they were waiting for something – and I knew what. I uncapped "Bruce Daniels" and we all had a toast right there in the hall.

MY COLLEAGUES

My colleagues at Moscow State University almost universally hold both their undergraduate and graduate degrees from Moscow State. In the United States, Harvard and Yale are top-heavy with Harvard- and Yale-trained scholars, yet also have many faculty members trained elsewhere. Every Moscow State history professor that I met had a Moscow State Ph.D. – every single one. And most of them have not gone somewhere else and then been hired back after achieving distinction. The decision to hire them is usually made when they are finishing their doctorates. Jobs at Moscow State are not advertised and then competed for by several candidates. The chair, the dean, and a few senior professors simply agree among themselves that each year, a small number of their truly superior new Ph.D.'s should be asked to join the faculty on a five-year contract. When a department such as history has more than 200 members, it can absorb quite a few new members each year and the problem of "academic incest" or "cronyism" does not trouble anyone. Invariably, the response to my questioning of hiring practices is that (1) Moscow State is the best school in the country, so there is no reason to hire products of a lesser place; and (2) the various candidates are extremely well known and Moscow State does not get the unpleasant surprises that some American schools do when they hire relative strangers.

Russians, by the way, call the entering degree for professors a Ph.D. only for the benefit of westerners. Among themselves, the accomplishment that comes after four or five years of successful graduate school and culminates in a book-length thesis is called their "Candidate's Exam." It is certainly equivalent to a doctorate in a North American university and is the union card needed for university teaching, as the Ph.D. is in the West. Russians, however, reserve the term "doctorate" for use among themselves to refer to an accomplishment that one achieves later in life, usually in one's late forties or early fifties. This doctorate is awarded by those in the department who already possess it, to a person who has continued to be very productive as a scholar and presents a mature piece of scholarship – perhaps his/her third or fourth book – to these peers, who may award the doctorate based on this seasoned scholarship. In many ways, this Russian doctorate is equivalent to being promoted to what in the West is referred to as the status of "full professor" – which in reality is "professor" without the preceding words "assistant" or "associate." Most Moscow State history professors do not have this Russian doctorate, and most never will. Nevertheless they are expected to continue to be (and invariably are) active researchers as well as teachers.

My colleagues have a light teaching load – usually one or two classes per term – but almost all of them have a heavy advising schedule because all students write long, detailed theses; they all take part in admission and final exams, which are entirely oral and thus very time-consuming; and they all sit as members of committees that write the textbooks used in hundreds of other universities in Russia and former Soviet countries. Additionally, virtually all of them have part-time jobs, most often serving as tutors or translators, because they are paid horribly by Moscow State. No one can live reasonably, let alone comfortably, on the pittances that professors are paid in post-Soviet Russia. Salaries range from $100 to $500 per month in a city where the cost of living exceeds New York's. Without outside jobs a professorial life is impossible; with outside jobs it is still not very comfortable. The low pay, of course, is one reason why Moscow State and other universities can hire so many professors – it does not cost the schools as much to hire three professors as it would to buy a copying machine. And professors get the status of their distinguished university affiliation, which does raise their fees in the tutorial and translating fields. Nevertheless, though this arrangement makes life possible, everyone agrees that it does not bode well for the future of higher education.

So my colleagues understandably complain and yearn for the good old days of the Soviet Union when professors were well compensated and enjoyed a higher social status. The West's criticism of the negative aspects of Soviet Communism – political repression, censorship, and economic inefficiency – is understandable and justifiable, but this criticism also obscured some of the Soviet accomplishments – education among them – that were quite extraordinary. Czarist Russia had one of the least educated populations in Europe; before the Revolution, most Russians were illiterate and the country had but a handful of universities. By the end of the Soviet Union, 98 percent of Russians could read and write; top-flight university educations were offered freely to the best and brightest of students on a genuinely competitive basis; and research in medicine, science, and the humanities proceeded on a world-class level. The ballet, the arts, and state museums everywhere supported cultural awareness and advances. The price for all of this was a lack of freedom in some areas of expression that I would consider too high a price to pay – but this does not mean the educational achievements were not very real and very much to be admired.

By every account, education has suffered tremendously at all levels in the transition from a public to a private economy. It really does remind me of that wonderful Kris Kristofferson line in *Me and Bobbi McGee:* "freedom's just another word for nothing left to lose." In the name of freedom, education has been cut loose from public support, and nothing has stepped in to provide it with a meaningful replacement that can pay professors and teachers a living wage so they can do their job and educate future generations. The new Russia values commodities by what they cost. Education simply is not being valued by this society, and unless something is done – and done quickly – the gains of a near-century of educational growth will be wiped away, and a new age of ignorance will darken the brightest light of modern Russian history.

Thus my colleagues despair, complain, and do their best under very bad circumstances. I share their frustrations. One of the strangest student demonstrations that I have ever heard of suggests that students also share their professors' frustrations and realize that if the faculty continues to be paid so poorly, students will suffer in the long run. On April 12, about 4,000 students rallied in central Moscow in support of education, with signs that dealt primarily with low professor salaries. One read: "How About Trying to Live on a Salary of a Young College Professor?" And another: "Enough of Dumb Reforms – Remember College Professors." I have never heard of North American students holding a rally to protest the low pay of their professors, and I doubt if I ever will.

Many of my colleagues have another avenue of support and another historic tie to the past that also makes them remember much of the Soviet era with nostalgia. My sample is small because I did not become close friends with large numbers of professors, but of those that I did get to know, all seemed to have been remarkably well connected to the old Soviet Communist Party bureaucracy. Irina Kruleva (a name eerily close to my student Irina's, the "old-fashioned girl"), a young scholar in her mid-30s who like me specializes in colonial American history, was assigned by the department to help orient me to my classes and students. We became good friends and I got to know her family and background. Her grandfather, a general in World War II, had sufficient stature to be buried within the Kremlin walls—an extremely rare honor. Her father and her much older brother both retired from the Red Army as colonels at a time when the army enjoyed immense prestige, high pay, and exalted status. Irina lives in a spacious central Moscow flat, has a new car, dresses beautifully, and, of course, does this all on her low pay and cobbled-together tutoring jobs. Clearly family money plays a major role in her ability to live as she does. Her family would not be wealthy by North American standards, but they clearly were and are privileged beyond average Russians.

Another good friend, Maria Troyanofskaya, is in her 50s, a historian of modern America, and is full of fun. She is divorced with two adult children and drives an old car with dents on the dents, in which she wheels around Moscow with the confidence of an Indy 500 racer. She dares to park anywhere she wants. Sidewalks, crosswalks, boulevard lawns—they hold no terror for my pal. Maria did not tell me of her family, but others did. Her grandfather was the first Soviet ambassador to the United States, her father had often served as Stalin's translator and had been the Soviet ambassador to the United Nations during the troubled times of the Soviet war in Afghanistan; both Granddad and Dad had been ambassadors to Japan. The two are buried near Khrushchev in Novodevichy ("New Maidens") Cemetery—second only to the Kremlin Wall as a distinguished resting place for dead Soviets. Maria's former husband was also a high-ranking United Nations official, and she lived in Geneva for eight years, which she described to me as "real boring."

My third best friend among colleagues, Yuri Rogulev, whom you will remember greeted me on my arrival, has a slightly less exalted background but nevertheless a status that substantially elevated him above the norm. His father had been an orphan who had risen through hard work, acts of heroism, and undoubtedly great ability to the rank of colonel in the Red Army. Dad was buried in a regular cemetery, not the Kremlin Wall or Novodevichy, but a Red Army colonel would be a person of substance.

My fourth chum in the department, Ekatherina Romanova (Kata, her friends call her), a young professor in her mid-30s who specializes in international relations and is a close friend of Irina's, has less high-ranking parents, but nevertheless they were well-placed, university-trained engineers. Although neither of her parents were in the army or diplomatic corps, they both worked on military/defense projects all of their careers. As with so many defense workers, they have suffered a decline in status and pay since the end of the Soviet Union.

Among other colleagues whom I met but did not get to know more than in passing was the grandson of Vyacheslav Molotov, of "Molotov cocktail" fame, and the daughter of Nikolay Sivachev, the great scholar whose name is attached to the chair I occupied during my Moscow stay. The elder Professor Sivachev, in addition to his great scholarship and much-talked-about charm, had also been head of the Communist Party organization at Moscow State.

The high social status of the background of so many of my colleagues suggests to me that Moscow State faculty used to be somewhat born to their jobs in the way that Oxford and Cambridge professors used to be. Succeeding in all three of these universities required great ability, hard work, and character, but the confidence that sometimes leads to these qualities occurred more naturally in people who were raised in situations that made them comfortable with decision-making and decision-makers at a high level. I would not want to suggest, of course, that the history department had no professors who had arisen from humble circumstances, but the high status of so many members seems undeniable and not accidental. Irina and Kata also say that educated, relatively affluent, and culturally aware families start providing for their children at an early age the tutoring and training that enable them to pass the rigorous entrance exam.

As far as I could tell from casual conversations about professional matters, my colleagues were every bit as able and knowledgeable about American history as were my colleagues in the United States. However, I have
almost no way of assessing the quality of their research scholarship
because virtually everything they write is written in the Cyrillic alphabet
and published in Russia. Every colleague who has published a book has
traveled to the United States for much of the research, and this gives me
some confidence in the quality of the work, but uniformly the books are
remarkably short – 100 to 150 pages – which I find a bit worrisome.

Also, most of these books are never reviewed in an academic journal or
a newspaper, not even once, and this raises some concern about whether
they are meaningful contributions to an ongoing, evolving scholarly literature, or just so many notches on a professorial academic belt. The number
of copies published seems tiny – usually about five hundred – but then
again, I know that many academic books published in Canada have similarly small press runs. Most of my colleagues' books are published by Moscow
State on the recommendation of Professor Yazkov and other senior people
in history, and this causes me concerns, too, about the inbred quality of the
judgments being made, but once again I realize that it may be unfair to
expect American procedures in a Russian world. In sum, I fear that these
books have extremely little influence outside the smallest of circles, but I
admire the commitment to scholarship that Moscow State historians
vouchsafe throughout their careers under extremely trying circumstances.

One area where I found my very accomplished colleagues and my brilliant students to have a strange lacuna in their knowledge was in American popular culture. This is somewhat true of all foreign scholars of American history, but much more true for Russians than it is for the French,
Germans, Indians, Pakistanis, or Brazilians, to use just a few examples. In
the Soviet era, American films, novels, television – all the trappings of U.S.
mass media culture that were such popular imports in most places – did
not penetrate much behind the Iron Curtain. Thus, to my great surprise,
when I gave a talk to the history faculty about the impact of the trashy
novel *Peyton Place* on the image of the small New England town as a center
of morality, I was shocked to discover that not a single one of these
learned scholars had ever heard of it. My colleagues could debate the effi-
cacy of town-meeting government, describe the Northwest Ordinance's

plans to lay out towns in the post-Revolutionary American west, and wax indignant about municipal corruption's effect on poor immigrants in the Gilded Age, but they had not heard of *Peyton Place, I Love Lucy,* the Three Stooges, Katharine Hepburn, John Wayne, *Gone with the Wind,* Hula Hoops, *My Fair Lady,* O.J. Simpson, and so on. How could a person be so familiar with the United States and American history and never have heard of O.J. Simpson? Easy, when none of the news coverage of American entertainment and trivialities was available.

This makes teaching difficult because I realized that so many of the images we use in the classroom to illustrate something historically are drawn from modern popular culture. This difficulty is rapidly waning because in the new Russia, current American situation comedies are shown nightly on television with dubbed Russian dialogue. The benefit of Americanizing Stalin's great-grandchildren with episodes from *The Simpsons* or *Friends* is subject to debate, but it will make teaching history here a bit easier for my successors. Alone of American culture, only rock-and-roll music somehow managed to infiltrate the Russian ethos in the era from World War II until the early 1990s. Rock cannot be stopped—not by anybody or any government.

In sum, after getting to know the faculty and students over a long, intimate semester, I found that the extraordinarily positive impressions that I had formed from meeting the Yazkovs and my student, Irina, were reinforced by every other single part of my contact. Quite simply put, Moscow State University is a glorious jewel of education. Its faculty and students perform at a remarkably high level and deliver equally remarkable service to Russia—and they do so humanely and with a wonderful sense of community and duty. All of this is at great risk, however, and if financial support continues to wither for facilities, faculty, and students, Moscow State's quality will plummet—and once it does, it will be unlikely ever to rise again to the level it has long enjoyed. Everything that I heard from my colleagues suggests that the same story can be told about virtually every other university in the countries of the former Soviet Union. This is particularly sad because the new freedom of expression that former Soviet scholars now possess could be used to polish the education jewel they have inherited. Instead, poverty is tarnishing the former sparkling university system because adequate private resources are not forthcoming to replace the government funds that have been lost.

CHAPTER TWO

Walking Around Moscow
What a Guide Book Won't Tell You

Moscow has that immediate look and feel of a big city much like New York, London, Paris, Rome, Hong Kong and Buenos Aires. Not many cities have it: as much as I love Boston, it does not; Toronto is getting close but is still not there; I would have to be persuaded that Chicago has it; but no one walking in central Moscow would need an ounce of persuading that Moscow is a big city. Founded in the twelfth century, it has approximately twelve million inhabitants, and was the capital of Russia until the late eighteenth century, when pro-Western forces within Russia made St. Petersburg the capital. After the Bolsheviks triumphed in the Revolution of 1917, they restored Moscow as the capital. Changing it again would be unthinkable to most Russians.

Moscow was bombed frequently during World War II, but thanks to the large land barrier separating it from Germany, advance warnings and good anti-aircraft defenses helped spare it from the aerial damage suffered by cities such as St. Petersburg. Remarkably few Muscovites were killed in the bombing because in addition to advance warnings and skilled ground defenses, the deep tunnels of the Red Line subway – the only subway built before the war – provided secure bomb shelters.

The land battle for Moscow, however, was ferocious, and German troops penetrated to a point between Sheremetyevo Airport and the city: the spot is commemorated by a series of giant metal cross-beamed structures lying on their sides that one drives by on the way in from the airport. Moscow's defenders placed similar obstacles across fields and roads because they effectively blocked the tanks' progress.

Stalin had the city rebuilt immediately after the war and created Moscow's most noticeable buildings: a series of seven large, neo-Gothic skyscrapers with layered tiers, whose outlandish size came to symbolize Soviet-era architecture. The buildings, variously called the Seven Sisters, Stalin's Wedding Cakes, and Stalin's Sisters, now have differing uses. Two are hotels, two are apartment blocks, two are government ministries. One of these, the Ministry of Foreign Affairs, is on Smolenskaya and visible from my door; the final Sister is the flagship building of Moscow State University. It is on the highest hill in Moscow and is the most distant from the city center but still probably only seven kilometers from my flat. It is absolutely stunning – all seven are – but as my historian friends lament, it is the scientists who gave the world Sputnik and Soviet preeminence in so many technological areas who were allowed to move in to this architectural wonder. The Kremlin and St. Basil's Basilica, Moscow's other two most famous landmarks, are famous for their beauty throughout the world and justifiably so, and Red Square is one darn big and impressive square. Lenin's tomb is still there. A number of beautiful museums abut the Kremlin area. With the exception of the Sisters, most of Moscow is a low relief of six to eight stories.

In addition to the Sisters, Stalin created two other unusually successful additions to the city that have transformed it: subways and underpasses. Before the war, the Red Line, constructed in the 1930s, was the only subway line. New lines have been steadily added every decade and now the eleventh is partially open as construction nears an end. No one lives more than a stone's throw from a subway station. Not only is the metro – Muscovites use the same short name as Parisians do – the most easily accessed subway in the world, it provides the best service at the lowest prices and is the most beautiful. Trains run every minute or two for most of the day, and every three or four minutes at night until 1 a.m. They are clean, cost less than fifty cents U.S., and some of the stations are positively beautiful. Rich or poor, everyone uses the metro in Moscow, and no one ever complains about it.

The second addition to the modern transportation system is less artistic and technologically demanding but also adds immeasurably to the ease of getting around. At all the main squares and on all the main streets with a high volume of traffic, pedestrian underpasses allow walkers to cross dangerous terrain safely. Hundreds of these underpasses make walking life so much more pleasant than it is in many other cities; some main streets have one on every block, and they give access to all four corners of the block. Each underground walkway is full of small shops, which number in the tens of thousands.

CONSUMERITIS

But skyscrapers, great public buildings, museums, the metro, the underground passageways be damned – the single item that jumps out at you in central Moscow today is that this old capital of the world's greatest socialist state is absolutely awash – I mean swimming obsessively – in consumerism. *Buy, buy, buy* at every turn you take, whether you are walking on Red Square or in an alley too small for cars. Neon signs, billboard ads, artful window dressing, thousands of human billboards walking the streets wearing sandwich boards: the volume of the sales pitch is deafening, and the range and price of goods is staggering. This is not the Moscow I visited in 1993 as a tourist when a traveler could make a profit by selling blue jeans to a local hipster. Everything in the world is available here and being hawked ostentatiously before your eyes. Abutting the non-Kremlin side of Red Square is a gorgeous old brown building of three large stories that has a cantilevered glass roof much like those of traditional train stations in nineteenth-century western Europe. On the first floor, the stores are a Who's Who of opulent retail: Hugo Boss, Louis Vuitton, Burberry, Christian Dior, and their ilk. The sum total of all these extremely tasteful, beautifully arranged shops adds up somehow to an immense vulgarity. Who can afford these goods? Most tourists cannot. Tourists go to the GUM (as this department-store complex is called) but they do not buy much and instead gag at the prices. Yet the stores were busy and someone was buying all of these obscenely expensive things. The buyers speak Russian and are, indeed, Russian. But who are they and where do they get the money? Surely none of them are among the government clerks who were demanding that their salary range of 2,000 to 4,000 rubles per month ($80 to $160 US) be raised by 10 percent; surely these clerks did not save $600 to pay for a Liberty scarf. My colleagues at Moscow State all shrugged and looked hopeless when I asked them who kept these stores open.

The answer lies in the new wealth created in the years since the end of the Soviet state. Old Soviet enterprises were sold off at fire sale prices, making thousands of instant multi-millionaires, almost all of whom live in Moscow. Even more productive of immediate and big fortunes, the incredibly vast natural resources of Russia – the oil, gas, and metals – are being pumped and pulled out of the soil in international transactions that mystify the smartest of people working at normal jobs, and mystifies also much of the government bureaucracy which is now trying to put a stop to the situation after much of the genie is out of the bottle. The people shopping in these luxury stores are the relatively few who have either, depending on your point of view, (1) shown themselves to be the new successful capitalists that Russia needs, or (2) looted the country through licensed criminal economic enterprise.

But it is not just the rich who view consumerism as the new sport. Everyone wants to play the game, even if only at the most minor league level. Everywhere one goes in Moscow, the buying and selling of Western goods, from Levis to Clinique cosmetics to all the various designer labels, confronts a person; it is like a never-ending mall experience. Conservative Americans might be inclined to ascribe this excessive acquisitive impulse to demand that was pent up during the Communist era, but that seems far too simple; something happened to this country on the road to the market revolution that made many people giddy with and about goods. My colleagues at Moscow State did not seem to share this shopping mania, and I am sure many other Russians do not. One age group, the old or retired people living as pensioners, is sadly left out because its members lack entirely the means to stay alive under acceptable conditions, let alone to find a Ralph Lauren polo shirt or a Benetton sweater at a bargain price. The market revolution has impoverished Russia's oldest residents, who probably have a more negative view of capitalism than Lenin ever had. I have never seen a city – not New York, not London, not Paris, centers known for consumption – that chases Western goods as aggressively as Moscow does in the post-Communist era. I was amazed.

THE ARBAT

Ironically, the street that symbolizes commercial Moscow to visitors and residents alike – the Arbat – is the most "touristy" stretch of retail real estate in the city, yet it remains beloved by locals. Over a kilometer long and closed to vehicular traffic, the Arbat is akin to Bourbon Street in New Orleans or Beale Street in Memphis, except that those two places are almost exclusively populated by out-of-towners. Despite the ubiquitous

souvenir kiosks on the Arbat, at least 90 percent of its strollers are Muscovites who eat and drink at the fifty or sixty restaurants and cafés that line
the sides. Accordingly, the food is often good and the prices, although
high, are not outrageous: bargains for tea, beer and shashlik (Russian meat
shishkabobs) are easily found, and every Muscovite seems to have his or
her favorite Arbat place to share with a friend. Even on the coldest days of
winter, a few sturdy buskers can be heard, and in general, a nice, warm feeling of gaiety characterizes the street even in the most frigid weather.

Many of its buildings are pastel and resemble those of St. Petersburg
more than the rest of Moscow. On several side streets are tiny museums
often devoted to local artists or writers or artistic movements of whom or
which I have never heard: I also would never have heard or known of the
little museums were it not for my ever-helpful students. My flat was a five-
minute leisurely walk from one end of the Arbat, so I meandered down
this little slice of Russian urban charm at least once a day and usually
more. Midway down on one side is the requisite statue of the great
Pushkin – the literary figure whom Russians revere beyond all others.
Pushkin is posed with the wife whose honor he died defending in a duel
against a villainous Frenchman, who robbed the country of at least fifty
years of literature from its most beloved son. Across from Pushkin and his
wife is a statue of Bulat Okudjava, the late twentieth century poet and balladeer who immortalized the Arbat in verse and song. Posing for pictures
with tourists were two men, one of whom was dressed and groomed to
look exactly like Czar Nicolas II and the other like Lenin. Between being
paid one hundred rubles for instant camera snapshots, the Czar and
Lenin played chess; the game looked serious and not intended to be a
joke for the audience. The Arbat has a biker joint which usually has twenty or so Harleys outside; the bikers ride their hogs and choppers to this
pedestrian way via an intersecting side-street and then wheel them by foot
into parked position. Some artists sell pictures of Russian scenes they have
created for export to living rooms in the West; others try to talk people
into a quick portrait for three hundred rubles. Men and women of all ages
hold hands, nibble snacks, and drink beer as they stroll and talk; women
push baby carriages; school children chase each other; businesspeople
walk quickly through and are clearly on their way to a meeting or work but
choose the Arbat as a route because – well, because it is the Arbat.

The Arbat had one busker who stood out above all others literally and figuratively. He was extremely tall and gaunt, had soulful eyes and long hair, dressed in black coat and hat rather like Johnny Cash, and played a strange stringed instrument that I am certain was his own creation. It produced a beautiful, sad, wailing sound that was something like a cross between a steel guitar and a harp. Such was his renown that other musician/buskers often stopped to talk to him and examine his instrument, and local café owners turned off their piped-outside music when he stationed himself near their patios. He was quite talkative between songs but while playing seemed to go into a near trance. He usually moved every hour and played in about four different places a night. Alone of all the buskers, he seemed to do very well financially for obvious reasons – he was gifted and charismatic. My guess is that if he continues to play as he does for a few more years that he, too, at some point will have a statue erected to his memory. It seems to me that I have been watching a legendary balladeer in the making.

As you can tell, I love the Arbat. Despite its commerciality and its appeal to tourists, it is so unlike a mall. The Arbat was my home away from Moscow home. Using it as a point of departure, I sought to explore Moscow with students and friends in order to learn the city's stories that do not get told by guidebooks. Consider this a quirky man's tour of a few famous and not-so-famous places that are caught in the cross hairs of historic, Soviet, and capitalistic Moscow.

THE BEAUTIFUL OFFICE BUILDING AT LUBYANKA. An imposing, extremely attractive, nearly square nine-story building dominates Lubyanka Plaza, which sits one block and a three-minute walk from Red Square. Fortress-like, the building has gray brick on its first two floors and yellow brick on the next seven, and is one of the most visible office buildings in the city. Tens of thousands of people walk by it each day or catch the subway at its metro stop or shop in one of the stores on other parts of the plaza. The gray-yellow brick building is an intimate part of Moscow and seems woven into the flow of daily life. It was the KGB headquarters in the Soviet era and is now the home of the KGB's successor, the FSB (sounds too much like the FBI, does it not?). Of all the infamous Soviet institutions, nothing chills the spine as much as the one that had those initials –

KGB. It strikes me as incongruous that the KGB headquarters building should be so pretty. One thinks: God knows what went on in there. It strikes me as strange that it should be so exposed to every citizen, tourist, spy, terrorist, or dog who walks by; why isn't it hidden away somewhere in a secret bunker? The most secretive agency of the world's most secretive government should not be a charming landmark located in the hustle-bustle of bargain-hunting shoppers and rush hour. But it is. Go figure.

ST. BASIL'S CATHEDRAL – NOT THE KREMLIN. Ivan the Terrible caused St. Basil's to be constructed between 1555 and 1561 to commemorate Russia's victory over the Tartars at Kazan in 1552. St Basil's is beautiful beyond belief and almost no one gainsays this opinion. In gratitude for his artistry, Ivan had St. Basil's architect blinded so he could never duplicate his masterpiece. Fairly clearly, Ivan did not come by his nickname for no reason, although blinding an artist may not have been his worse crime – he also killed his son.

Almost all Americans recognize St. Basil's four large and four small brightly colored domes even if they usually do not know the cathedral's name. It is the Russian building most known to Americans and the western world. Why? St. Basil's is located at the southeastern side of Red Square and adjacent to the Kremlin Wall. Whenever television journalists reported on any event from Moscow during fifty years of media-covered Cold War, they used St. Basil's as a background but would sign off saying: "So and so, reporting from Red Square." The cathedral was ubiquitous and many Americans mistakenly believe that St. Basil's is the Kremlin or is part of the Kremlin. Not that associating the Soviet-era Kremlin with religious cathedrals would be wrong; a stone's throw away within the Kremlin walls are three other beautiful cathedrals grouped around a small courtyard called the Plaza of Three Cathedrals. These three are in the Kremlin – which is just a Russian word for fortress – but St. Basil's, the symbol of the Kremlin to much of the world, is not.

RED SQUARE. Of course, Red Square is not a building but rather is a famous landmark, the one westerners used to watch on Soviet holidays when thousands of soldiers, tanks, and ballistic missiles trooped past the leadership of the Communist Party while Kremlin analysts used the occasion to forecast who was rising and falling in the Communist leadership ranks. The square is indeed beautiful and large, but most Americans and Canadians associate it so strongly with menacing weaponry and Communism that it brings a bit of a chill to the spine. The name – Red Square – seems to say it all. But the name has nothing to do with Communism and predates the Russian Revolution by at least three centuries. The name comes from two sources that are mutually re-enforcing. Merchants who gathered in the square in the sixteenth century often built fires for heat during evening trading hours, giving the square a red hue. Additionally, "red" means beautiful and pure in Russian: Until Russia followed the western traditions initiated by Peter the Great, Russian brides traditionally wore red to get married. So, Red Square was red literally and it was beautiful according to its name – and it still is.

THE WHITE HOUSE – YES, THAT'S RIGHT – THE WHITE HOUSE. All Muscovites and Russians know this building, which has offices for some of Russia's most important governing bureaucrats and parliamentarians as "the White House." It gets this unofficial name partly from its white color, but even more than that, from a puckish sense of humor by those who wished to spoof the United States. Built in the mid-1980s, the White House is quite attractive and is located on the Moscow River, about two kilometers from the Kremlin. It is not a terribly important building today, but in the late Soviet era it was the main meeting place of the Supreme Soviet and thus, briefly, was important. The nickname might not have survived had it not been for two famous incidents in modern Russian history that played out on western television in front of the White House. In the more famous, in 1991 Boris Yeltsin faced down Soviet tanks as some generals tried to mount a coup against the reforming government of Gorbachev. Two years later, the new president, Yeltsin, bombarded the building with tank fire to chase out deputies opposed to his ascent to power. Now it is a tourist attraction and for the foreseeable future will always be known as The White House.

THE HOUSE ON THE EMBANKMENT. A large, ugly, sprawling gray series of buildings on the Moscow River and within easy sight of the Kremlin, the House on the Embankment is not an official name but it is the term commonly used to describe what people always say was an unhappy place. Built in the 1920s as a complex with its own stores, a school, and other amenities that made it a virtually self-contained urban village – including the first indoor toilets in Moscow apartments – the House served as living quarters for the highest-ranking members of the Communist Party, Soviet government, Red Army, and their families.

Why is such a swanky place always described as unhappy? Late-night knocks at the door often signaled disgrace, imprisonment, or death for many of the House's residents. It remains a symbol of Stalinist purges; a small museum in the complex today shows why the image is so deserved. The museum shows the House's walls that were honeycombed with crawl spaces where KGB and other security agents eavesdropped on residents to gather any intelligence that could be perceived as being disloyal to Stalin. Despite their sumptuous quarters, few residents of the House had happy lives or bright and long-lived futures.

Almost all the House's residents in its heyday were aware of their precarious situation and of the constant scrutiny under which they lived. One can imagine a comedy-show skit on late-evening conversations between husbands and wives – "Oh aren't we lucky to have Comrade Stalin for our supreme leader, dear?" "Yes, indeed, my darling. I would follow him through the deepest snows of Siberia and never question his judgment; he is the world's best revolutionary" – but, of course, the real scenario could hardly have been funny.

Today, the House still functions as a little urban village with stores, restaurants and even a theater in its midst, and the apartments are still among Moscow's best and have a stunning view of the adjacent Kremlin just across the river. But it is known as a place of bad memories. All humor about the place, however, is not lost: A trendy restaurant in the basement of the House is outfitted as a Soviet spoof with grim waiters, a spare décor, and martial music from the 1930s. Alas, the prices are more current.

METRO STATIONS. My favorite Moscow buildings, bar none – because all of them have some nice detail and many are so original – are the more than one hundred metro stations. Built in the Soviet era with the exception of a few currently under construction, the metro stations all have lovely, dark wooden benches on which to sit, high ceilings, marble floors, and hundreds of chandeliers and elaborate wall lights. Many have high arches throughout and thematic art built into them. A station just two stops away from my stop on the Blue Line, for example, is devoted to the Revolution and has hundreds of brass figures carved into the walls that are meant to symbolize various kinds of sacrifice. University students from all over the city go to this metro station to rub the nose of a certain dog in one of the carvings; somehow the tradition developed that doing so will bring good luck on the exam. Not surprisingly, the pooch has a shiny nose. Other stations are not so political, although the Soviet hammer and sickle is everywhere in them. The station named Mayakovskaya, after a Russian poet, has fifteen ceiling domes, each of which is decorated with a beautiful mosaic. My favorite is a huge station, Kievskaya, which has approximately forty large frescoes and mosaics in the central hall, depicting Russians in various productive activities: harvesting wheat or pitching hay dressed in colorful peasant clothes, working in a factory, studying in a classroom, building a hydroelectric dam—you get the idea. The pictures are beautiful, detailed, brightly colored, wholesome—and, above all, they are proud.

CHRIST THE SAVIOR CATHEDRAL (or The World's Holiest and Largest Swimming Pool). The Romanovs built Christ the Savior Cathedral, Moscow's largest church, to commemorate Russia's triumph over Napoleon. Located adjacent to the Kremlin Walls in the city center, the Cathedral fell into ruins after the Bolsheviks came to power and they eventually had its dome torn down and a huge swimming pool installed within its foundation walls. This seems particularly sacrilegious even for the atheist Soviet Communist Party. In 1997, Moscow's Mayor, Yuri Luzhkov, a big thinker and eccentric politician about whom you will hear more later, had the cathedral rebuilt at the staggering cost of $350 million. Many Muscovites, outraged by both the costs and the size of the domes, which they consider gaudy and horribly oversized, say that they prefer the old swimming pool.

PARK ISKUSSTV. What does a city do with all the statues of political figures that are no longer in political favor? Where did Iraq put all those hundreds of Saddam Husseins? Did they all get destroyed? We know that the Taliban destroyed Buddhist statues for political reasons and that

Cromwell's Puritans destroyed all sorts of religious icons in England. Moscow had a somewhat different answer for some of the local statues of gentlemen made unpopular after the end of the Soviet Union. They dragged many of those toppled from pedestals in front of buildings or in the center of squares to Park Iskusstv, which was already an outdoor art gallery. So, go to Park Iskusstv now and see the first head of the KGB, who used to reign over Lubyanka, or see a few old members of the Politburo who are immortalized in bronze and have a new but crowded resting place.

MONUMENT TO PETER THE GREAT. Zarub Tsereteli, the architect who designed the reconstruction of Christ the Savior Cathedral, created Moscow's strangest new monument, a huge statue of Peter the Great. Everything about this monument is ridiculous. First of all, Peter the Great so thoroughly hated Moscow that he created the new city of St. Petersburg and made it the country's capital. Erect a statue of the big guy in St. Petersburg, but not Moscow. Second, the statue is butt-ugly and makes no artistic sense: it is too tall for its base, is a nondescript, boring brown, and shows Peter standing as a mariner before a mast (He did modernize the Russian navy and loved ships). Many Muscovites tell the same story about the statue: they argue (and seriously) that Tsereteli had been commissioned to cast a giant statue of Columbus for an unnamed American city, and that when the city rejected his creation on aesthetic grounds, he renamed it Peter the Great and got his pal, Mayor Luzhkov, to buy it for Moscow. This of course cannot possibly be true, but the inglorious location of the statue adds credibility to the tale: it stands unceremoniously in front of a chocolate factory on the bank of the Moscow River in a place distinguished by nothing. It looks as if Peter the Great were just plopped down on this spot for no good reason at all – which seems to be the case.

I acquired most of my own visual knowledge of Moscow during the winter when the constant ice cover on the sidewalks made rapid walking a bit hazardous. Warm-weather walking is vastly easier and reveals a substantially different city. All cities with cold winters and warm summers change characters dramatically when life becomes livable without central heating. The pent-up feelings that Winnipeggers call "cabin fever" propel pale-faced claustrophobics to spill outdoors in search of the natural world from which they have hidden for months. In late summer and early fall, the knowledge that winter is on its way makes many of us embrace the outdoors with a desperation that only pre-ordained doom can bring. European cities change from winter to summer behavior even more dramatically than North American ones because Europeans in general have smaller houses and flats and live more of their lives in public than do North Americans. But, as the growth in outdoor dining and cafés in American and Canadian cities shows, we are catching up to our more sophisticated ancestors.

However, I have never seen a city that transformed itself between cold and warm weather as much as Moscow did. Flowers absolutely bedeck every square inch of empty space: highway and river banks, window boxes, the middle spaces of the boulevards, planters on street corners, store windows – it is a floral paradise. Even in the winter, Muscovites love flowers, and one often sees a person scurrying along in the cold who is protecting a vulnerable and expensive bouquet of tulips tucked under the arm. But in warm weather the love can be, and is, particularly indulged.

About mid-April, the Arbat suddenly hummed with rotary saws and hammers as every café started building its outdoor patio. By May 1 they were all open for business. The number of buskers increased exponentially every day in May. I may be reading too much into this transformation, or I may just have gotten too used to store-clerk behavior, but I would swear that people smiled more at strangers in the warm weather and let down their guard upholding the non-involvement principle. As I said earlier, Moscow's winters are not that severe – nothing on the order of the legendary stature they have assumed internationally – but I believe that local residents may believe their own press and think that they are escaping the most cruel winter season known to man or beast. Whatever the reason, Moscow revels in the new spring and it brings out the best and the happiest in the city. Additionally, there is a lot of spring to enjoy because Moscow is so far north (it sits nearly astride the fifty-fourth parallel, which it shares with the middle of Hudson Bay in North America). By early June, it stays daylight until 10:30 p.m. In St. Petersburg, much farther north, the residents refer to this as "the season of white nights."

In addition to happiness, warm weather offers walkers the opportunity to see much more of the people of Moscow.

CHAPTER THREE

Life on Moscow's Streets
A World Capital Like No Other

All Muscovites agree that Moscow and the rest of Russia are separate worlds in which people experience remarkably differing lives. Moscow seems to be the place where the new Russia – for better or worse – amplifies all the trends that are sweeping the old Soviet empire. According to virtually all of my students, the rest of the country dislikes Moscow, envies Moscow, fears Moscow, and blames Moscow for everything that goes wrong in their lives. Moscow has an image in Russia much like New York City's in the United States, but few Russians get to visit Moscow. Many more Americans visit New York, and a visit invariably lessens most Americans' suspicion and hostility towards the city. Moscow does not have as great an opportunity to let firsthand knowledge soften its image among fellow citizens. Moreover, unlike New York, Moscow is the seat of national government and hence also reaps the additional negativity that in the United States is siphoned off to Washington.

Because of Moscow's power and visibility, demonstrations abound on its streets. They did also in the Soviet era, but of course these were all government sponsored and orchestrated. That part of the West's story on Communism was quite accurate – the freedom to criticize the government did not exist. It does exist now, although there are more limits than in the West, and the government still does organize demonstrations of support by pressuring off-duty police, clerks and other functionaries to turn out for pro-government rallies. However, groups of people take to Moscow's streets on their own these days, sometimes much to the government's discomfort. Some of these demonstrations reflect more than the new freedom available to the citizenry; they often show a wry, puckish sense of humor.

In February the Communist Party, ironically now a party of the belea-
guered opposition, organized a huge rally to protest the Putin government's replacing of many important benefits for pensioners—guaranteed
free medical care, unlimited free public transportation, greatly reduced
home utility bills—with a cash payment. By all accounts, the cash pay-
ments are inadequate and these old pensioners who expected a meager
but guaranteed *soupçon* of dependable care in their later years are now
being left to enjoy the benefits of a free market, which for them means no
benefits at all. Under the rhetoric of freedom and choice, the most
defenseless citizens of the new Russia were being skewered.

Editorializing aside, the protests themselves were more interesting
than their causes. The Communists and old people mounted a massive
demonstration at Pushkin Square, which was countered by a massive pro-
government rally and the two sides were yelling what I could only assume
to be incredibly nasty insults at each other. No one was happy. Then, from
the base of the statue of Pushkin, Russia's most beloved poet, fifty or so
people held another much smaller third demonstration, replete with
huge banners. I had no idea what the banners said but all the jeering,
screaming bystanders in both camps starting looking at the new protestors and talking to each other and eventually everyone seemed to laugh as
if a great joke dawned upon them. I went home completely perplexed
about what I had seen until *The Moscow Times*, a small English-language
newspaper, reported the story the next day. The protestors in the little
demonstration carried signs saying, in effect, "Mr. Putin, please make life
hard for us." "Mr. Putin, please take away our prosperity." "Mr. Putin,
please make the winter last forever." And on and on with these strange
requests. According to these demonstrators, the government always did
the opposite of what the people wanted, so they were asking for abusive
treatment in an obviously mocking and affectionate way. Both sides loved
it, and I did too, once I understood the message.

The second demonstration took place the next day and also at
Pushkin Square—a favorite place for demonstrations, and in this case very
appropriate, because it involved the memory of Pushkin. A French citizen
killed the great Pushkin in a duel in 1837, but this year on the anniversary
of the tragedy, a cadre of Pushkin devotees mounted an anti-French
demonstration. They called for sanctions against France because of this

dastardly blow to Russian culture inflicted by the French citizen. My bet is
that the French would not only respect this but, being the romantics they
are (or like to think they are), they would join in with the Russian mourn-
ers if they had a chance. Pushkin, by the way, comes up immediately in all
conversations about Russian literature, and everyone says the same thing:
Dostovefsky/schmesky, Tolstoi/schmolstoi, if you want to know the soul
of Russia, forget those guys: Pushkin, Pushkin, he's your man. And then,
they will go on always to say that he was one-quarter African black; somehow this is thought to be important for any American to know.

At about the same time in mid-February, another demonstration of
sorts–one that involved street art–made a whimsical mark on the
Moscow landscape. As you will recall, I arrived in Moscow as a great blizzard (for Muscovites) dumped tons of snow on the streets, which the city
was poorly equipped to remove. Everyone complained about the slow
pace of removal. Walking down the Arbat, I came across thirty or forty
well-styled snowmen two or three days after the end of the blizzard. The
snow persons stood in front of a theater on the wide pedestrian walkway.
Over the next month, they grew to be a snow crowd and eventually num-
bered well over two hundred. The snow people stood in lines, gathered in
circles talking, appeared to constitute a small choir, and in general just
looked to be the residents of a large snow village. They started getting old
metal buckets for hats, tree branches for hair, carrots and coal for noses
and eyes, and a couple even became rowdy and had beers in their hands.
Passersby brought their cameras to be photographed with their snow
friends and in particular, they took pictures of children snuggling up to
Frosty and Frosta. Then one day, they were gone; after about four weeks
they vanished overnight, presumably a casualty of the city's slow-moving
but unforgiving war on the snow world.

The snow produced another quixotic battle, not on but *about*
Moscow's streets, between Moscow's colorful and gutsy mayor, Yuri
Luzhkov, and the weatherman, who turned out to be a tough counter-
puncher. After a spate of horrible weather that had not been expected,
the mayor came out swinging in early March against a villain everyone
loves to hate – the weatherman. Mayor Luzhkov held a news conference to
propose fining the weatherman for being wrong so often. According to
His Honor, Moscow's weather service is wrong far more often than their

counterparts in any other major city, and Muscovites should not have to live with this incompetence. More than inconvenient, bad weather forecasting costs the city much money because officials cannot develop appropriate schedules for snow removal. His Honor did not seem to be kidding but appeared serious about the fines. He may also have wished to deflect the criticism directed at the city government for its appalling inefficiency in clearing the sidewalks and streets. His Honor may not have found the snow village as amusing as most Muscovites did.

The weather service director fought back in an unusual way but probably took the only tactic possible. He admitted that the weather service had a dreadful record compared to other cities but turned the finger-pointing around and blamed the mayor for forcing the weather service to work with hopelessly outdated equipment because the city has not properly funded the weather people. Pow! Take that, your Honor. The director further said that he would meet with His Honor and would accept the principle of fines on two conditions: (1) that an acceptable level of funding for new equipment be forthcoming; and (2) that the weather service people get good-work bonuses for accurate forecasts. Mr. Director clearly was no pushover.

And then, when the weather got a bit better as spring appeared, the whole storm seems to have blown over (so to speak). Perhaps His Honor and Mr. Director shared a bottle of vodka and watched the tulips sprout on the Arbat.

Another street scene, more earthy than whimsical, also showed the capacity of people to laugh at themselves. A restaurant close to Smolenskaya named – I kid you not – the "Moo, Moo" has a statue of a large Holstein cow in front of their window as an advertisement, and given the name, it is a perfectly appropriate symbol. The cow is not well proportioned artistically and has an udder that would be the envy of the herd, sporting four outlandishly large milk spouts (you get the idea). Often, people will pose with the cow; men especially will pretend to be milking Bessa (all Russian women's names end in "a"; my daughter Abigaila told me, and she is right). Invariably, these milkers look like farmers and my bet is that the vast majority of the men who pose this way have a great deal of firsthand knowledge of how big a cow's teats should be; they are country folk visiting Moscow and cannot wait to show their pals back home a picture of themselves milking a Moscow cow. The Moo Moo is a small chain with six other Moscow locations, so presumably this scene is played out in several places.

GLOBALISM. Not only is there a lighter, more frivolous look to life on Moscow's streets in the post-Soviet era, the city's residents have entered the international network of social and economic behavior in significant ways. Although a tired cliché, the term "globalism" accurately describes a very real phenomenon, and anyone who has traveled internationally over the last quarter-century will attest to the impact globalism has had on homogenizing tourist services, shopping, and street signs. The same shampoo can be bought with the same credit card in the lobby of a hotel in the same hotel chain in all the major cities of the world. One does not have to be an international economist with reams of data to know that we have become one big retail village. In Moscow, I have observed two signs of global culture. One is quite prosaic but, far more than the United Nations, may hold the answer to uniting humanity around the world in one fundamental activity – particularly because it characterizes teenagers and young adults, our next generation of leaders. The other sign is poetic, arises naturally from some deep loneliness within the human soul, and appeals to the other end of the age spectrum – the elderly, and particularly old men.

MALL CULTURE. So help me God, I could take ten Manitobans, Bostonians, and Texans, blindfold them, spin them around, and drop them off in the underground mall adjacent to Red Square, and they would not know that they were not in Canada or the United States until they heard Russian being spoken and saw the signs in the Cyrillic alphabet. Nothing washes away international cultural distinctions like the mall, and something in the DNA of young people allows them to instinctively assimilate mall culture until it becomes imprinted in their marrow. They have the same slow walk; they drift in and out of stores without ever buying anything; the boys poke each other in the ribs and shove each other by the shoulder; the girls put their heads together and giggle at exchanged secrets; both boys and girls gravitate to the same fried food in the food courts; and they do not notice any other human being over the age of twenty-four.

Where do the instructions for this behavior come from? Who knows –

but origins miss the point. Mall culture is here, and the U.N. should devise some way of incorporating it into international peacekeeping and nation-building operations in the future. Perhaps little mall symbols could be used to show that certain places are sacred; perhaps mall exchanges could be worked out between countries. Forget the Peace Corps – send the most experienced mall dwellers abroad to "underdeveloped" nations (the ones with puny malls). At the very least, the U.N. should appoint an Undersecretary for Mall Affairs right now so that the agency and bureaucracy is ready for the forthcoming generation of international mall-trained adults.

OLD MEN AND DOGS. I perch under my window every morning and night and drink tea while looking over the Moscow River and a little park that runs between my apartment block and the river. Most of the humans I see are walking dogs. The dogs come in every imaginable size and age, but the vast majority of the walkers are old men, although of course not all are. Invariably, the walking follows the same pattern. The dog is kept on a tight leash as he/she and the walker cross the highway to get to the park; the dog is straining in anticipation and the walker is restraining; and then, once the park is reached, the walker reaches down and unhooks the dog who bounds off into the snow for twenty yards and then comes bounding back to the walker who reaches down and ruffles the dog's coat around the neck; "good boy, good girl," is being said in Russian.

Then the dog runs away another ten yards and pauses to assume the telltale squat that means a poop is coming. Moscow refuses to implement a pooper-scooper law, so the old men have no unpleasant dung-removal work to reduce their joy. This absolutely poetic scene is repeated endlessly in front of my third-floor window and yet remains charming every time. It makes me happy to know that people can so love the company of an unspeaking but loyal friend, that they venture out into the freezing cold and feel absolutely well-compensated when they see their friend bound off joyfully and then come running back for a hug. City people around the world love their dogs – New Yorkers and Torontonians as do Muscovites – and undergo great inconvenience just to see that happy frolic. Keeping a dog in the country is easy and seems almost natural; keeping one in a big city is a pain in the butt, and yet city folk do it in huge numbers despite the expense and bother. It is a selfless act and one that the United Nations might also want to consider as it devises ways to promote international brotherhood. Perhaps thousands of dog-walkers could be sent to troubled countries instead of soldiers. Who would attack an old man waiting for his dog to poop?

And a little more on Moscow's dogs: they are everywhere. Moscow has 30,000 to 50,000 stray dogs, the most of any European city and perhaps the most in the world. This fact came out as the city government under the influence of its irascible leader, Mayor Luzhkov, postponed implementing a bill that would attempt to regulate the dog population, stray and otherwise. Before Mayor Luzhkov – who is clearly a dog lover – the city euthanized strays, but under His Honor's administration, the pound only sterilizes them. Because it is estimated that pet owners who cannot afford to keep their pets turn seven thousand additional dogs loose each year, the stray population is growing larger, not smaller.

More dog data from the same hearings: the most popular breeds in descending order are Caucasian Shepherd, German Shepherd and Labrador. Estimate is that each year, five to seven kilograms of dog poop are left per square meter in Moscow residential neighborhoods. And, yes, you guessed right: His Honor is against a pooper-scooper law.

MOSCOW ODDITIES. Some aspects of the profile of Moscow's population, however, do not conform to global standards. Moscow must be by far the "whitest" capital city or city of twelve million people in the world. I saw virtually no black people on Moscow's streets, and very few Chinese, Japanese, or Indians. People with Asian features can be seen in small numbers and invariably they are from the new republics in central Asia that have devolved from the defunct Soviet Union. Moscow has five or six Indian restaurants and maybe twice that number of Chinese restaurants – a mere drop in the bucket in a city so huge. It is, by and large, an extremely homogeneous city. The most common ethnic restaurants are Georgian and Uzbeki; both regions are renowned locally for their spicy food.

By all accounts, Moscow has a large population of prostitutes, but I did not see a single street prostitute even though I am a single male who spent six months walking the streets. I believe that I would have been approached by women selling sex in almost any other western European or North American large city. Prostitutes advertise their services as "escorts" in *The Moscow Times*, and apparently all the hotels that cater to westerners, about thirty major ones, have prostitutes in their bars and lounges – but there are none on the street. This is a fine thing but surprising, especially given Moscow's current rough-and-ready reputation and its consumer-driven ethos. Prostitutes are discreet.

A few other oddities struck me about Moscow's people. Russian women must either change brassieres four times a day or wear three at a time, or a lot of stores will be out of business soon. I have never seen so many stores that primarily sell women's lingerie. Perhaps Russian men wear them in secret but, if not, Russian women clearly pay a lot of attention to their bras and knickers. Perhaps Moscow lingerie stores are like candy stores once were in the United States – fronts for bookies or other illegal activities.

Second only to lingerie stores are the purveyors of cell phones. Cell phones are, of course, ubiquitous on this planet and although they are obviously handy, they may be the single most annoying piece of social rot in the twenty-first century: very few people seem to feel any compunction about intruding on the privacy of unwilling listeners. In North America, a few noble constituencies held out against this electronic blight – most notably university faculty members – but even they have largely given up the fight, and one hears errant ring tones at faculty meetings. All students, of course, have had them for a decade. Be that as it may, Muscovites use cell phones even more than their North American or European counterparts. It may well be that cell phones are the variable that best predicts how far a society has advanced on the continuum of consumerism. Notwithstanding, Moscow still has too many cell-phone stores; they cannot all possibly survive even on abnormally high cell-phone usage.

So, by carefully combining the cell-phone data with the lingerie excess capacity, I have arrived at yet another Daniels theory that possibly explains everything: *late at night, after all the westerners go to bed, Muscovites stand around in red bras and panties and talk to each other on cell phones.* Little else can account for the retail landscape. Whether Russians outside of Moscow are in on this practice or not, I cannot at this time say with any degree of certainty. If the above theory is not correct, the data more tamely – but surely – reinforce my earlier arguments on the highly advanced state of conspicuous consumption in Moscow, as well as the capacity of this new economic milieu to call forth an avalanche of small-scale entrepreneurs to satiate the latest hunger. Like American gas-station owners in the 1930s and video-store owners in the 1980s, most Russian lingerie and cell-phone kiosk owners will learn a cruel lesson about jumping onto a crowded economic bandwagon.

Some aspects of Muscovite behavior require less analysis than the surplus of lingerie and cell-phone stores; they are also more delightful. Most young people are tattoo-less. I saw very few tattoos on people, but they will be coming down the pike because I did see newly opened tattoo parlors. If Muscovites kick into high gear on tattoos they way they did on cell phones, this will change dramatically in the next two or three years, but at present the tattoo rate must be one-twentieth of North America's. Also I did not hear any recognizable version of the word "fuck," which I thought had grown to be a universal expression of something – not contempt, it is used far too casually – but the expression has not come to Moscow English unless it is so disguised that I could not hear it. This is the first place that I have traveled in my life and not overheard that word by people speaking English. The absence of tattoos and the casual f-word raised Moscow substantially in my esteem.

Beer is everywhere. At 10:45 a.m. as I sat in the window of my favorite café one morning, I watched a crew of six Moscow city workers clearing snow and noticed that at least four of them were drinking beer as they worked. They were not being surreptitious and hiding what they were doing but drank away freely as hundreds of citizens walked by. Students going from a class to the metro will drink a beer as they stroll along. Beer-drinking on the street is entirely legal and more than one-third of the beer sold in Russia is consumed on the spot. I know what you are thinking: Is there not a downside to this beer ubiquity? Are there not a lot of drunks on the street? Is not alcoholism a serious problem? Yes, to all of the above. I realize that one has to counterbalance the joy of omni-present beer drinking with some undesirable consequences, and alas, the bad probably outweighs the good.

If Moscow has more street beer than any American or Canadian city, it has many fewer street beggars than North America's largest cities and has none of that strange blight of well-dressed teenagers saying, "any spare change, mister?" Moscow does have beggars, however, and they tend to be either very old ladies who wait near metro entrances or former military men missing limbs or dreadfully disfigured who appear on metro cars, give a little spiel, and then wheel themselves through the car. Both the old ladies and veterans usually do fairly well, and one can of course understand why.

Moscow may have a short supply of street beggars, but it has street musicians galore. These buskers play everything. Not surprisingly, a sizeable number are teenaged boys with guitars who cannot carry a tune or master a chord. But at the other end of the talent spectrum are people who play violins, cellos, concertinas, and accordions with the ability of professionals – and indeed many of them are students from Moscow conservatories. And people play unusual instruments or instruments seldom played by buskers in North America: African flutes, the saw, full drum sets, and strangely stringed devices. Many play in the metro or the metro passageways but many others on the streets. Not surprisingly, buskers spring up like crocuses in warm weather, but even in the worst of winter weather, some are always in the metro. In the spring, the Arbat just popped with freely given concerts every fifteen to twenty meters.

I found a few aspects of Moscow's human culture to be maddening. I could not hide that I am not Russian under any circumstances, and it drove me crazy. I know, of course, that usually all Europeans can spot an American a mile away. But my parka was of the same look and vintage as most men I saw; I wore dark pants, a hat, and boots or shoes like Russian men's; I did not wear sunglasses since most Russians do not; like others I scurried with my head down during snow storms; yet every time I walked down the Arbat, all the souvenir shop hawkers called out to me, *"souvenir, souvenir."* How did they know?

On the streets of Moscow kids wear clothing showing every Western brand name, but they do not wear American sports insignia – it seems to be the only Western affectation lacking – with one horrible exception (at least for a true New Englander). One sees the New York Yankee stylized logo everywhere on shirts and hats – including heavy winter hats, for which it seems highly inappropriate. I asked a student wearing this sign of the Devil if he knew what it stood for; he did not and thought it just another American brand name. Is there nowhere a New Englander can go to be rid of this dreaded curse?

CAR CULTURE. I did not drive a car in Moscow, but if I did, I would be infuriated by the following manifestation of the civic non-involvement principle. Strangers do not go to the aid of any poor schlep whose car is stuck in snow and spinning its wheels to get out. In Winnipeg or Boston it is a violation of a sacred social contract to walk by a car in such a predicament and not give a push. In Moscow, fifty husky young men will stroll by a marooned car and give nary a glance. Somehow, this willingness to allow your fellow human to remain stuck in a snow bank for hours when a ten-second push will bring him or her freedom seems to be an act of unusual cruelty.

Car culture in general does not reflect glory on Moscow's population. Many nations or cities claim to have the world's worst drivers – New York, Boston, Rome, Athens, Calcutta, and Lisbon among them – but I am certain that if all the residents of those auto-maniacal towns came to Moscow for a weekend, they would unanimously concede first place and be forced to argue among themselves for second spot. Muscovite motorists absolutely refuse to relinquish any claim of right of way to pedestrians. They shoot across side streets to main boulevards without slowing down from full city speed, even though pedestrians will be crossing the side streets. It is unbelievable. In New York and Boston, pedestrians and motorists often play games of chicken as a walker steps in front of a car at the corner. Here no one does because it seems a certainty that the car will not stop. Cars have the undisputed right of way, and pedestrians must wait and beware.

Everyone acknowledges the problem, and one popular explanation is offered by all. When Moscow's driving culture was created, important people had cars and the rest of the population did not. Thus, the high social status of drivers gave primacy to the car. Drivers refuse to concede this primacy despite the democratization of car ownership. Another case of history being abusive to good sense.

A secondary variable also seems likely. Since few Russians had cars until ten years ago, the country has a huge percentage of new drivers. Think of your own wanton recklessness when first you got behind the wheel, and then realize that most of the drivers here have the experience of North American teenagers.

And yet a third variable helps to explain the auto mayhem. Bribery of driving inspectors is rampant, and no one with an extra two thousand rubles need fail the test. All of my students claim this is true and not just myth. I believe them.

Accident data support my (and all Muscovites') contention that cars are very dangerous here. Annually, Russia averages 19.4 deaths in traffic accidents per 100,000 people, compared to 11.9 deaths in western European nations.

Other aspects of auto culture are equally or more dangerous. Look out at a busy Moscow street and invariably you will see a pedestrian, male or female, hold up a hand and one of the next five cars will stop. The flagger will talk to the driver through the window and may or may not hop in the car. Every car on the street is a potential private taxi. The pedestrian will ask the driver if he/she is going to or near a specific place and, if the driver says yes, they quickly agree or not on an appropriate fare. Usually drivers will not charge much but will not go much out of their way. This economic exchange helps the driver pay for a little petrol for the daily commute and also makes money sense for the passenger who pays a fraction of a regular taxi fare. It is economical, and of course exceptionally dangerous – but Moscow is a dangerous place and only the vigilant survive unscathed. Westerners are warned never to hail informal cabs and obviously, if one does not speak Russian, it is virtually impossible to play the game.

VISIBLE HEALTH. Almost every negative in Moscow can be balanced by a positive. If people drive horribly and take dangerous chances with taxi-hitchhiking, if they drink far too much, if they eat too much smoked meat and cheese and not enough greens and vegetables – all of which I believe is true – nevertheless, they look healthier than North Americans do because they do not have our problems of obesity.

Commenting on people's physical appearances is risky because (1) it is very subjective; and (2) it can sound mean, judgmental and value-laden. But I would like to run the risk because a couple of details have struck me so forcefully that I think they are empirically verifiable, reveal something of Moscow, and are of consequence for the health of Russian and North American societies.

Most importantly, there is virtually no childhood obesity here. I have seen hundreds of children at play and scarcely any chubby ones. This healthy condition continues into young adulthood. None of my twenty students – not a single one – appears to be overweight. I could never make a similar statement about a class of twenty North American students I taught.

The above seems to me to be beyond any questioning but what follows is more subjective. My sense is that somewhere in their early thirties, many Muscovites do get pudgy but not fat. A general stoutness seems to characterize middle-aged and older people, but almost never does one see an immensely obese person as is so frequently seen in North America.

On the other hand, in North America, amidst the many very obese, one sees men and women with no body fat and rippling muscles that are obviously the product of frequent, disciplined gym workouts. I have seen none of these in Moscow. In North American cities, gyms have sprouted up everywhere and people jog in every park. In Moscow, the only gyms appear to be in hotels for travelers and I did not see a runner in my entire stay.

I have no basis to comment on what produces the weight differences between North Americans and Russians other than what you and I and every North American have been hearing on the news and reading in papers since the epidemic of obesity first became a matter of public discussion.

Any health benefits for the Russian population that result from having less of a weight problem are, of course, offset by the much greater incidence of alcoholism and traffic injuries. Moreover, Moscow is – as one of my colleagues told me – a "smoker's paradise" because one can smoke anywhere and cigarettes are incredibly cheap. Not surprisingly, 64 percent of Russian adults smoke, compared to 28 percent of English and 20 percent of Americans. All signs indicate that the health of Russians has declined sharply in the years since the end of the Soviet Union. The most recent vital data are amazing to me: for every two births, there were three deaths; Russian men live an average of sixty-three years, fifteen years less than average American men. Life expectancy for all Russians was sixty-seven years in 2005; the comparable figure for the United States was eighty-one.

One piece of health data the government released was genuinely shocking: the army reported that approximately 25 percent of all deaths of military personnel in the last several years were suicides. This does not sound like a good datum for recruitment ads.

Let me end this description of life on Moscow's streets with a little vignette that is both a little sad and also a little funny in an odd way. Little blue portable toilets with the word "toilet" still written on them have been "liberated" by many vendors who operate souvenir kiosks, knickknack stores, or news stands. The outdoor entrepreneurs have turned these portable-pots into little refuges to escape from the cold wind. They sit on what once was a toilet seat with the door open and can leap out to do business and then retreat to their sanctuary. As are shopping carts in North America that are used by poor people for a variety of other purposes, these toilets obviously are all stolen, but the police do not seem ever to bother the users. Many of the portable toilets are in their intended use, however, and for the going rate of ten rubles, one can use them for relief.

CHAPTER FOUR

Scenes from Everyday Life
The Perils of Living without Language

I have frequently traveled overseas without benefit of being able to speak the language. As a matter of fact, unless I go to England or Australia or one of the few other places where English is the mother tongue, I will be experiencing a language-free environment because sadly enough, I am, like most Americans, monolingual. It is embarrassing to be so limited, but the truth is that it is not the insuperable hardship one might think, because a small number of people speak some English in almost every corner of this planet, and, if not, one can always gesture and beg and throw oneself on the mercy of local host nationals who more often than not are extremely kind to a pathetic soul wildly waving arms and loudly repeating words that make no sense.

Few Russians that I met in stores or my neighborhood or on the metro spoke any English, although that is changing. Young people are learning English today in Russia because it is the best language to know for international success. Thus, if I desperately needed the help of an English-speaking person, I always looked for a well-dressed person under the age of twenty-five who had the look of a student. My students at Moscow State all spoke perfect English, of course, or else they would not be my students, since I taught in English.

Compounding the difficulty of living without benefit of the local language is that one is speechless at precisely the time when one has most need of explanations for various things. It would be easier for me to be mute in Boston, Winnipeg, or San Antonio, where I understand fairly well how the world functions, than to be speechless in Moscow, where many aspects of economic and social intercourse are new and mystifying to me. Nevertheless, not once did I find myself so frustrated by being unable to communicate verbally that it ruined my day or mood. If people can laugh at themselves and do not mind appearing a little goofy, they can survive virtually anywhere without knowing a word. This goofy guy did and enjoyed many good giggles while doing so. I have tried to give below a sense of some of my everyday travails and triumphs that occurred in Moscow *sans lingua*. Most of these vignettes of daily life I have tried to put into narrative form for maximum impact. Those that I have described virtually as they were occurring I have left in the present tense.

MEET THE KEYSTONE COPS

I was strolling down the Arbat on my way home about 5 p.m. after getting a tea in one of my new hangouts and feeling exceptionally carefree. Two police approached me in broad daylight and one said, "Mister, mister, papers."

Now of all darn things, I did not have my passport because it was at the Ministry of Education, which took three weeks to register my visa. All visitors to Russia must have their visas registered within three days or get in big trouble. For tourists, it is no big deal because every reputable hotel will register you when you arrive; presumably the hotels send the government a list every night of all the visas they have registered. The government is incredibly but understandably obsessed with security concerns and wants to know where every foreigner is at every minute.

For visitors like me on non-tourist visas or for anyone (again like me) not staying in a hotel, the process is dreadfully complicated. My landlord must certify the visa for the non-hotel part; this is a big pain for him, but counterbalanced by the knowledge that foreigners pay higher rents. Anatoly has done his part. However, for the work part of my visa, the non-tourist part, my employer, Moscow State University, had to issue me a letter of invitation before I came to Russia; then after I was in Russia the appropriate ministry, in this case the Ministry of Education, had to register the visa also. The Fulbright people hired Alexey to do all this and gave him the usual instructions because, of course, they know the drill well from experience, although it apparently is always changing. The Ministry, however, required my passport and at the moment, they had it, while I had an official note given me to carry around until the passport with the properly registered visa would be returned to me.

"Mister, mister, papers."

What to do? I took out the official note and showed it to the one policeman – militia, they are called – who spoke very little English.

"Mister, mister, what is this?"

The "i" in all the words is pronounced as an "e" so it sounds like "Meester, meester, what ees thees?" I tried to explain but nothing seemed to be understood.

"Mister, mister, no picture" (again with the "ee" for "i" in "picture" as well which made it sound like "peekture," alternately humorous and threatening).

I thought it would probably be inappropriate for me to ask my interrogator why he sounded a lot like a Mexican border guard. So I showed him my Texas driver's license, which of course does indeed have my picture and my name.

"Mister, mister, no good: how I know what this is?"

He had a point there but I knew that he knew my first document was entirely good and was all that I should need. I say nothing.

"Mister, mister, where you living?"

"Over by Smolenskaya," I answer truthfully.

"Mister, mister, what street address?"

Now this is weird and a little embarrassing, but after two weeks I still did not know my address because I could not read the street-sign that was written in Cyrillic letters and my apartment door had no number on it and my block seems to have no name. I told the cop that and he looked genuinely surprised.

"Mister, mister, we got leetle problem."

Again I say nothing because I have nothing to say. Meanwhile his friend has moved away and is harassing two other poor souls who look too dark to be Russian nationals but have the advantage of speaking Russian.

"Mister, mister, I don't want your little problem. How we make go away?"

I try to look confused but I think I know where he is headed.

"Mister, mister, it is my friend's big day," pointing towards the other cop. "You understand? It is the day he was borned. If you buy him cognac or vodka, the little problem go away."

By now enough time has passed in this charade that, although I am still a bit scared, the whole Abbott-and-Costello quality of the situation has made me more amused than frightened. I am taking part in performance art. So I respond.

"Well, why didn't you say so right away? Of course I'll buy you and your pal a drink. Where can we go?"

Again, a bit of honest surprise on his face.

"Mister, mister, you give rubles and we buy drink later."

I thought that I should not push my luck and I did want to go home.

"Okay, how much do you need?"

"Mister [only one mister] maybe one thousand rubles?"

I want to say, "So where's the second 'mister?'" but I realize that I am in the midst of negotiations and sarcasm might not be good for my bargaining position.

"I don't have a thousand rubles."

"Mister, maybe three hundred?"

Now I take my wallet out again and start looking for three hundred rubles, but the birthday boy excitedly calls something to my pal, who runs over to his buddy and the other two victims. I stand there alone for thirty full seconds and finally shout something over to the little group; my pal calls over, "Mister, mister, you go home."

So I did.

WHAT DID I LEARN FROM ALL THIS? Well, I have been hearing stories about frequent police shakedowns from many people, but I had been a bit skeptical and assumed that they could just as easily have been the stuff of urban legend as of reality. I am now a believer. I also learned that I wanted my passport back as quickly as possible and I felt much better when I had it tucked away in my pocket. My guess on the ending of that little situation is that the other two guys did have some genuine problem with their documents and this made them more lucrative prospects.

GETTING CABLE TELEVISION

I am embarrassed that I could not live without television but I do plead professional necessity because I had a difficult time staying on top of American and world news. My newspapers were limited to *The Moscow Times* for which I was grateful and the *Herald Tribune* when I could get it, but I am a news-aholic and I felt deprived. Moreover, my students continually peppered me with questions about current American politics and foreign policy. So, enough of the apologies – I wanted CNN in English and it was available fairly cheaply, about $50 a month. One channel is all that I got for my cable hookup, CNN International, but it was fine.

Arranging the hookup, however, was something else.

My Moscow State colleague, Irina Khruleva, handled all the details for me and scheduled the cable-man to arrive between 10 a.m. and noon and for my landlord Anatoly to arrive before 10 a.m. because he had to open the stairway to the roof for the cable-man to make the connection. Only Anatoly had the keys – or so he, Irina, and I thought. Anatoly arrived at 10:10 and through his gestures and obvious manifest symptoms, I gathered that he had been and still was very sick. Anatoly, who is older than I, trudged up the stairs to open the roof door but arrived back at the flat in five minutes with a look of panic. "Nyet, nyet, nyet," he kept repeating. I divined that something was wrong with the key: it was either broken, or the lock had been changed – Anatoly is one of many landlords who own flats in the building – or something.

So, what to do – the cable-guy would arrive at any minute and I had been waiting for more than two weeks. Anatoly now repeated, "Irina, Irina," and it was clear that the only solution was to pester my friend to translate for us. She has a cell phone so I called her and explained the problem. Irina talked to Anatoly, she then talked to me, and then we passed the phone back and forth as the desperately wheezing and germ-spewing Anatoly and I had a conversation through the good offices of Irina as translator, who was probably in the middle of something else in her busy day.

The problem was, indeed, that for some reason Anatoly had not foreseen that he could not get to the roof. He knew where a key was that would work, but he had to leave for twenty minutes to get it. During our three-way, pass-the-phone conversation, Irina told me several times that Anatoly was "slow," which is polite for not very smart. He actually seemed okay to me but I was only going by gestures. The new plan was for Anatoly to speed off to get the right key and then return posthaste. With any luck, the cable-guy would not arrive until Anatoly returned. Cable-guys in Russia – as in North America – were always late. If he did arrive on time, I had to delay him until Anatoly reappeared or I would be waiting a long time to move back up the list.

Thirty seconds after Anatoly left, the buzzer alerted me to the arrival of the on-time cable-guy. So he was not traditional in time management, but he was in every other way. He was impatient and wanted to get the work done and be gone. He spoke no English, but why should he? I was the one at fault because I am the guy who speaks no Russian and we were in Russia. He wanted to go to the roof because he pointed up. I countered by bringing out a teapot and pointing at it to indicate that I would like to make him a pot of tea. He looked very wary now, and probably assumed that I am gay. I had to admit that if I were pointing to the roof and the other guy disappeared and came back pointing to a teapot in his hand, I would think it a bit odd. If I had a bottle of vodka, I knew that I could point to it and succeed in the delay gambit, but I did not.

What to do? I absolutely hated to bother the long-suffering Irina but I had no choice. With cable-guy pointing more and more insistently upward, I again left him in the hallway and dashed back into the flat to call Irina. Thank God she answered – a less kind woman would have turned off the phone – so I ran out to the hall and guided cable-guy into the flat and handed him the phone which was not cordless so I could not bring it with me. Cable-guy probably thought I was going to mug or kiss him as I pulled him into the flat, but he came and then did talk to Irina.

She explained the situation and this time there was no need for a three-way conversation. I could tell that cable-guy was pretty darn unhappy but that he would wait. I could also tell from the clear international no-translation-needed body language that he would not wait long. He had to do some stuff in the flat also, of course, so he now rearranged the order of business and did that first instead of last. But cable-guy was good and cable-guy was quick and now he was done. What to do? Again I brought out the teapot. Again cable-guy declined but this time with no wariness or curious look, this time with a bit of surliness that I would guess might translate into "what kind of an American weenie does not have a good bottle of vodka on hand for emergencies?"

As luck would have it, Anatoly returned just a minute or two after cable-guy finished so he wasted less than five minutes all told. The two had a surprisingly lengthy conversation and I would not be at all surprised if the phrase "American idiot" was repeated in Russian several times by each. Both went up the stairs – I assume to the roof – and Anatoly returned in five minutes and sat in my (his) little kitchen while I typed this present description and cable-guy did his roof-work. My problems were over, I hoped, but I should have known not to count my Russian chickens before they hatched. Sure enough, cable-guy took far longer than the estimated ten minutes he told Irina was necessary, and when he came back to the flat, he opened a box of sockets for a wrench and talked animatedly with Anatoly. Something was wrong with nut sizes or something on the roof. My guess is that cable-guy told my landlord – maybe Anatoly is a bit slow – that the roof's hardware, like the rest of the equipment in the building, was from the 1930s. I did not know but I was too embarrassed to bother Irina with another phone call in which we could have a four-way conversation via pass-the-phone. No need: cable-guy – visibly sweating despite the fact that he has been outside on the roof in the middle of winter – headed back upstairs muttering something, my guess: "Man, that Anatoly is slow."

Fifteen minutes later, cable-guy returned and he and Anatoly had another lively conversation. The two were looking and pointing out the window in the kitchen but then cable-guy came into the other room where I, Mr. American Idiot, sat inscribing all of this, and cable-guy unhinged one window to open it. The windows had two hinges, however, one on top as well as one on bottom, and cable guy yanked at the window unaware that there was a top hinge that kept the window closed. He probably assumed that it was just frozen. I tried to say something, but of course what good was I? Anatoly, however, heard the noise and came running in and was not pleased at the potential damage to his property. Whatever. Anatoly unhinged the hinge, the window opened, and cable-guy leaned out precariously – this is the third floor – and looked up and down, back and forth several times each way for a good minute. He was not a happy cable-guy, but safely back in the flat, he again left for the roof. By now I began to think that my earlier embarrassment about wanting TV may have been a sign that I should have soldiered on in news-ignorance never knowing what George Bush or Ted Kennedy were doing until they made *The Moscow Times.*

Cable-guy disappeared a long time; Anatoly sat miserably in the kitchen and as I recorded all of this at the computer keyboard, I thought: what if cable-guy has fallen off the roof? I could not trust the slow Anatoly to make a proper report to the authorities, but would have to bother Irina again. I thought: will there be a happy ending to this story? Will I have hundreds of hours of watching CNN reports on Charles and Camilla or of Michael Jackson's trial, during which time this imbroglio will just be a funny story in my travelogue? Will there be an ending, or will cable-guy and Anatoly simply move in with me and the three of us can drink vodka all day? Who would need TV with comrades like them? I knew I was getting silly but I had to mark time somehow during cable-guy's very lengthy absence.

Cable-guy came back and had more conversation with Anatoly but it did not seem as tense. Cable-guy again tried to open the window, again forgot the top hinge, and then gave a little laugh when he remembered. I took this as a good sign but it also could have been a preface to enjoying thinking how far he could throw the American idiot and the slow Anatoly out this large window. Again cable-guy jumped up and left.

And then a new crazy development: ten minutes after cable-guy decamped for the roof, the feverish, unsteady, desperately ill Anatoly opened the window and leaned out, standing – which was even more precarious than cable-guy's leaning position – and yelled upward.

Cable-guy appeared within a minute and the two talked again but nicely.

Then cable-guy took off his coat, hat, and boots and it was clear that the roof stuff was all done. The next hour involved wiring a large box, fishing for the cable cord hanging out the window – the vacuum wand eventually did the job and using it was my idea. I suggested it by gesture and was mighty proud to be able to do something useful. Cable-guy had to drill a hole in the much-attacked window but he politely asked Anatoly's permission before doing so. I could tell that it pained my landlord to allow his property to be so injured but he did agree to it with a shrug. Anatoly probably wanted to go home as much as I wanted him to. The only other surprises were the paperwork. I had to produce my passport, and all three of us had several pages of forms to fill out. I signed – and I am not exaggerating – six different forms when all was said and done. I often had no idea whether I was entering the right information or not because the forms were written in Russian and I had to guess what was asked.

For a few days, I went on a drunken news-spree. For all his troubles, Cable-guy charged me only an additional 350 rubles ($14 US), which seemed unusually kind. He left smiling and probably felt sorry for the American idiot and poor slow Anatoly. I thought that perhaps cable-guy and I should go bowling some time.

WHAT DID I LEARN? In retrospect, at least half of the time that I have hired someone to do something at my houses in Winnipeg or Texas, the work has been more complicated than originally expected. Workmen in both these places also often justifiably considered me an idiot. Probably this little episode would not have seemed unusual or goofy were it not for my language incapacity and Anatoly's inability to have his apartment's hardware compatible with the modern era of nuts and bolts. The paperwork in Winnipeg or Texas, however, would not have required the death of a tree as the Moscow job did, and if I had spoken Russian fluently, the paperwork would have been just as extensive. Capitalist Russia has bureaucratic traditions that are holdovers from the Soviet era. Red red tape – so to speak – still rules.

DO NOT — I REPEAT — DO NOT EAT THE GRAPES

My hair had been getting a little shaggy and had not been cut since Hazel Love of Lubbock gave me a send-off trim about a week before I left. So I set out in search of what appeared to be highly elusive barbershops. Every big hotel in Moscow had a hair salon with stylists who spoke English, but these all charged an arm and leg, and if I wanted my hair cut this way, I would have stayed in Lubbock. I wanted a Russian barber in a Russian shop who charges Russian prices: I wanted a Russian haircut.

Ed Roslof of the Fulbright support office gave me directions to the barber he uses, who was tucked away in an alley behind one of Stalin's imposing Seven Sisters. Ed gave good directions and I found the shop, although I would never have known what it was had not Ed written out for me in the Cyrillic alphabet the word "barber." Alas, the shop was closed when I got there but I made a mental note of its exact location and felt the need to celebrate this small triumph by having a late lunch at a new café.

I chose a place with the unlikely name of the *"Cum Cum Kafe"* because it looked busy and charming. Inside, it was both and, as so often happens, after scrambling about and barking some orders, the *maitre d'* found a waitperson who spoke a little English, who was assigned to me. This young woman sat me down, responded to my request for a lamb kabob with a nod, and trotted off to place my order. The crowd seemed all Russian, well dressed and well mannered, and I was pretty happy with my choice. It was about 3 p.m., a typical time for Russian mid-day dinner, and it was my first meal beyond a plum and banana for breakfast, but I was not dreadfully hungry.

Each table in the restaurant was nicely set in western fashion except that each setting had a shot glass for the potential vodka toasting that is so prevalent. Each table also had a nice little basket of bread and a small bowl of fruit consisting of a bunch of grapes, two oranges, a kiwi, and an apple. I nibbled on bread until my platter of lamb shish kabob arrived; it looked good but was a bit more than I could handle. Joining the lamb were four potato pancakes and a little salad. I ate all the lamb, one pancake, and grazed on the salad and then asked for my bill.

I can tell already that you can guess what is coming. Yes, that is right: some cruel abuse was about to be inflicted on my daughters' inheritance. I sat there blissfully ignorant, munching a grape or two and thinking about what a lovely café this was. I was prepared for a big bill because I realized it was a classy joint, but I was unprepared for a bill this big, about fifty U.S. dollars, for a modest lunch with no alcohol. The lamb itself was about what I expected, $15, but the check had five other items on it and, of course, was written in a mysterious alphabet. I felt like a hick from the sticks when I asked the person who came for the money to identify each item, but darn, my English-speaking waiter had been replaced by this check collector who spoke only Russian. It became clear, however, that this restaurant was as *a la carte* as a restaurant could possibly be. The bread was expensive – and I only took two bites from a basket that was sitting there before I arrived; the bottled water was much more dear than a good beer – I suddenly noticed it was French; the little salad and the potato pancakes must have been house delicacies. I accepted all of this with a little sadness but resignation, but still was dumbfounded by the final item, which was 480 rubles or just about $20 US. This final item took the lunch from expensive to extortionate. Hick be damned, I wanted to know what it was and put my finger on the line to indicate my question to the increasingly impatient collector. She understood immediately what I asked and reached over to the fruit bowl and held it up. That's right; those four grapes cost me the twenty bucks and I now owned the rest of the fruit bowl.

WHAT DID I LEARN? Before my daughters say, "What a goof, Dad," and think how pleased they were not to be there to be embarrassed by my conduct, consider the following: I now noticed that fellow victims were every-where. On many of the tables of my fellow diners I saw the equivalent of little Russian doggy bags. What do you suppose was in those bags? Yup. Fruit. Other gouged patrons had decided that if they bought that fruit for that price, they were taking it home. My language incapacity and general cultural ignorance were not entirely to blame; people in the mainstream learned the same lesson I did. *There are no free grapes in capitalist Russia.*

This was an extreme example of a lesson that I had already been taught in a few lesser ways. Almost everything in Moscow restaurants has a separate price. In a pub where I have had a snack or two, the waiter always asked if I would like some bread, and I realized after the second time that the bread was a separate line-item cost and did not come with the meal. On the other side of the surprise equation, Russian restaurant bills, and indeed all other purchases, do not have taxes added on; the value added tax is already built into the price.

GESTURES DO NOT ALWAYS WORK

I still needed a haircut so I returned to the area of the grapes scam a full two weeks later as I was beginning to look as if I had my own built-in hat of wolf's hair. The barbershop was jammed with people waiting and I made a few introductory gestures by pointing to my head and going "snip, snip, snip" to a clearly snippy receptionist. She pointed the way to another room, which I entered to see four haircutters – three women and one man – and three other women that I gradually perceived were manicurists. I repeated the pointing and snipping routine since, although it had not endeared me to Ms. Snippy, she seemingly understood it. So, too, did the inside crew of workers and the nearest manicurist gestured that I should sit down. All four barbers had someone in their chairs, but as bad luck would have it the only man finished first and motioned for me to sit down. My bad luck was about to get worse because it very quickly became apparent that Mr. Barber had a dreadful cold. Having someone fuss with your hair for a good while is kind of intimate and I prefer a woman to do this but I especially prefer a healthy, non-sneezing, non-wheezing, non-nose-dripping person to be this close to my face for what would turn out to be forty-five minutes.

Mr. Sick Barber asked a couple of questions and I replied that I did not understand. He seemed like a nice guy and did not seem annoyed, but first pointed to my mustache; I understood that he was asking appropriately enough if I wanted this cut also. I did want the mustache trimmed, for it was bushy beyond anything I have had since the 1970s, but I did not want him to be inches away from my mouth and nose for several minutes with his millions of germs. So I shook my head no and he looked at me with disbelief but then asked something else. He gestured with his finger and thumb showing a gap of about an inch and then narrowing to about one-twelfth of an inch and I realized that he was asking me how much hair I wanted taken off – or I *thought* "taken off" was what he meant. I responded with a replying gap of my own and indicated by a very small space that I did not want to have too much cut off. I had noticed before coming into the shop that most Russian men had very short hair and I wanted mine to be longer. "Just a little taken off, just this much," I said as I showed the little gap. Saying anything made no sense but somehow I assumed – quite incorrectly as it turned out – that my words made my gapping signal more clear. Mr. Sick Barber responded knowingly, *"hdgt thvcyfgrh thffsy,"* and I nodded approvingly.

I now fully understand exactly how two intelligent (or perhaps only one in this case, and it was not me) people can interpret a piece of sign language in completely opposite ways. My friend Judith Graham has complained to me for several years that I get my hair cut too closely; thank God I will not see her for several months. By the time that I realized the crossed signals, it was too late, and one-half of my head had almost no hair on it. I think that I did not immediately see that he attacked my hair with the basic plan to remove most traces of it because I was so transfixed by fears of the germs that I tried to hold my breath when he was in front of me or close to me. But about ten sneezes and fifteen hand-to-nose wipes later, I realized that he had interpreted my tiny gap to mean that this was the length I wished my hair to be when all was said and done. And this is the length that it became. My head was not shaved but it was just one millimeter up from shavery. And now that I think about the sign language, Mr. Sick Barber's interpretation makes more sense than mine and I have only myself to blame.

He spent an inordinate amount of time nearly balding me and clearly took great pride in his work. When he was done removing most traces of hair, he again gestured to the mustache and again I refused. His very painstaking work proved to be a bargain: 250 rubles or about $10 US. Try getting your hair cut in Winnipeg or Boston or San Antonio for the price of a quarter pound of codfish. When you amortize the price over the number of months the haircut will last me–probably most of the rest of my stay in Moscow–the bargain becomes all the greater. I also learned that I could save additional money on shampoo. I needed less shampoo per washing.

The first thing I noticed on my walk home was that Moscow seemed a lot colder when a person had no hair on his head. Then I thought of an advantage to my new look: no danger of getting hat-hair. Not only did I need to wear a hat for warmth, I could now wear one also for cosmetic purposes and live without fear that removing the hat would reveal strange patterns my *chapeau* left on my scalp.

I had kind of hoped to get a Russian girlfriend while I was here but now it seemed unlikely that I would, unless I met someone who was inclined to like Nazis or skinheads. In a world of short-haired men, I became one of the shortest. Since the haircut, however, I came to realize that others might interpret my new look differently. Valia, the quite chic Russian woman who manages American-Russian cultural exchange pro-grams, said to me, "you look very stylish." I did not know her well enough to tell if she was kidding or serious. One of my students asked if I had joined the U.S. Marines.

Addendum to the haircut story: Surprisingly, after about ten weeks my hair grew back to the point where I needed another trim. I could have waited until I got home, but I accepted the wisdom that I had received a very fine haircut–just that it was calibrated in reverse length to my wishes. So, I thought that I would try again but be forewarned by my previous experience and make some preparations. To wit, I asked Valia to write a note for me as if I was a little boy going off to see the barber and carrying instructions from my mother: "Do not cut this man's hair too short: take off as much as will probably grow back in three weeks." And off I went to the same shop.

Ten weeks is a long time and I did not expect anyone to remember me; I hoped that I might get one of the three women this time. The former Mr. Sick Barber, now, thank God, looking just like any other male barber, either had the memory of an elephant or perhaps could always recognize his own scissor-work even in a hat-matted, shaggy state. Two of the three women were free, but Mr. Barber smiled broadly and gestured to me that

I should sit in his chair. He said something to the women that must have indicated a proprietary claim because they put up no fuss even though both had stood up attentively when I walked in.

Mr. Barber and I exchanged pleasantries as best you can when you have no idea what the other person is saying: I said, "hey, how are you? How's the hair-cutting business?" He responded: *"xhnsdhyfhdygnb, yhygfd, brghydhy,"* and then giggled at his own witticism. I sat down, he wrapped me in a cloak and tape around the neck, and then asked me *"lghdyn, pngs-by bidhgy?"* which I took to mean: "how do you want your hair done?" I gave him the note and our entire relationship changed in a heartbeat.

Mr. Barber called one of the other women over to his chair and showed her the note. He was not happy. She responded with a flurry of questions I can only imagine: "Did you butcher him before?" "Is he a pervert?" "Are you a pervert?" "Is he trying to destroy your professional reputation?" "Would you like me to stick my scissors in his neck?" Mr. Barber responded with longer and louder answers. I assumed that I was about to be passed to the woman when she went back to her own chair – maybe she refused – and a new personality emerged: Mr. Surly Barber went to work. No more pleasantries. No little friendly questions such as: *"hdgtyf, pjdnym dht?"* No giggles. No showing me my profile in the mirror. Just *snip, snip, snip,* and I was out of that chair in ten minutes. I thought of trying to make amends by pointing to my mustache for a trim but then I thought Mr. Surly Barber might shave it for revenge and feign ignorance.

The haircut was terrific, just the length I wanted and nicely done, but if I were doing it again – and I will not – I would not sacrifice such a beautiful friendship just for the sake of a good haircut. I have this mental picture of Mr. Surly Barber complaining indignantly to his wife and children at supper about the American idiot who had humiliated him by criticizing one of his haircuts.

WHAT DID I LEARN? Friends are more important than hair and some newly emerging professionals in Russia take great pride in their work. I predict a glorious future for Mr. Proud Barber: he has made a successful transition from communist to capitalist Russia.

WHEN GESTURES NEARLY FAIL

How much language does a person need to take a simple item – say a sweater – to the dry cleaners? Not much when everything goes right. You drop the item on the counter, the clerk takes it, gives you a receipt, you pay what he or she indicates by writing down a number, and then you come back, produce your receipt, and pick up your clean clothes. Pretty simple; who needs to talk? But what about when something goes wrong? This turns out to be a bit of a different story – stories need words.

I took a sweater to the cleaners and everything went as above except that the clerk produced a detailed document that rather resembled a contract a person gets when renting a car, where you have to initial four or five boxes to waive certain "protections" and then sign on the bottom line. I had no idea what I was waiving, but everyone in front of me in line had initialed similar agreements, so I did, under the reasonable assumption that I was immunizing the cleaners in case the sweater shrunk, colors ran, or the fabric got fuzzy. I initialed, paid 147 rubles (about $6 US), and the clerk pointed to a date on the calendar. Thus wordlessly, I went through the whole checking-in process without a hitch.

I am not a complete fool; I knew that if I lost the receipt I had a better chance of getting elected to the Duma (Russia's parliament) than ever seeing my sweater again, so I tucked it in my wallet very carefully. On the appointed day, I went back and gave said receipt to a different clerk who took it, scurried away, and returned with my dry cleaning. Now the full meaning of the contract that I had initialed became apparent. I discovered that I had agreed that if Russian cleaning fluid turned my navy-blue, lamb's-wool sweater into a God-awful purple necktie, the cleaners was absolved of all responsibility. Because that is what she brought back to me – the ugliest, cheapest tie that has ever been worn by any man in all of Europe. I had quickly to get past my first thought – *why would anyone pay to have such a piece of junk cleaned?* – because that was not the issue. Where was my sweater? That was the issue. Now I needed language and shaking my head, pointing at the tie, and saying *"nyet"* was not doing the job. Nor was it endearing me to the long line of people behind me who were waiting for their own purple ties. The clerk held the tie up to show that it was indeed clean and undamaged, which did seem to be the case. How to indicate that the tie was not mine?

I was wearing a sweater so I pointed to it, but this had no effect on the tie-waving clerk. The clerk was wearing a sweater so I pointed to it. This did have an effect, but not a good one. I think she took this as some sort of perverted American proposition: "Hey, baby, want to take our sweaters off together later tonight?" She is now mad and using her own gestures, which I understand to mean "Take your stinking tie and go away; I am too good-looking and young for you"—not true—and "I have a long line of other customers," which was quite true.

What to do? Do I take the tie and leave and come back with a Russian-speaking friend? If so, kiss the sweater goodbye and look for a shirt to match the tie next Halloween. She had the receipt and I would have no proof; it would be a different clerk and I would look like a fool—a sweaterless fool. So I persist. Now I point to a long list of items that the cleaners has posted, all of which have prices next to them. Despite my receipt's great length, apparently neither sweater nor tie was enumerated, but the price was, and my bet was that the two did not cost the same. I point to the list where it says 147 rubles and the clerk looks and then looks at my receipt. And then she looks at the list again. My guess is that the Russian word for sweater has 147 R next to it and that the Russian word for tie has something else. *Aha*. She scurries away and is gone quite a while; the line grows much longer and people are less happy and talking much among themselves. I really have to learn the exact words that translate as "American idiot" because I would bet big money that they are being repeated often.

The clerk returns with no sweater. All this time, by the way, the purple tie sits on the counter in front of all of us and I am sure the crowd is also saying, "Why is the American idiot complaining about his ugly purple tie? Who cares if the cleaners botched the job? Only an American idiot would wear such a tie." The clerk now picks up a cell phone and makes a loud call to someone. The line that might well be thinking of turning into a vigilante mob can hear everything the clerk says, and her words cause a discernible stir. I believe that at this critical juncture, the heat came off me and went on the cleaners. The clerk now reads numbers from my receipt—a lot of numbers—and then copies more numbers down. She scurries away for the third time and returns fairly quickly with what looks to be my sweater wrapped in plastic. I do not bother checking because my sweater or no, I am leaving while the leaving is good. I skedaddle. And I think the line understood that I was not an American idiot – at least not this time.

When I get home, I check inside the plastic wrap – it is my sweater and the cleaners did a nice job.

WHAT DID I LEARN? Sometimes a visitor has to stand and be counted even if he or she risks being called an American idiot. And, even in matters of commerce, the new capitalistic Russia displays some of the bureaucratic overkill of the old communist system. One sweater/tic requires an immense number of forms and numbers.

JUST GET ONE LITTLE WORD WRONG

At the request of the American embassy, I made a trip to the Russian city of Khabarovsk to give a talk to a conference May 11 and 12 on the subject of war and the nations of the Pacific. You may well ask why I was asked to go to speak on a subject about which I know nothing more than the average bloke in the street. Of course, it was not I, but the holder of the Sivachev Chair who was asked to speak, and it was the conference's bad luck to get a seventeenth- and eighteenth-century historian to speak on a twentieth-century topic. I did propose a talk that had some relevance and for which I was professionally qualified. I wrote an essay on the early intellectual origins of the concept that God is on the side of Americans and argued that the belief derives from the Puritan and American revolutions. This sense of Godly favor gives Americans an extraordinary belief in their own country's international goodness and in the United States' destiny to spread American values around the globe. Good or bad, appropriate or not, this was the best I could comfortably do and it seemed to do the trick.

But the talk I gave is not why I want to write about my trip to Khabarovsk. The one-little-word problem is the subject of this vignette. What is the word? Read on to find out.

Khabarovsk, by the way, vies with the more well-known Vladivostok to be the capital of what is called the Russian Far East. Khabarovsk is about seven thousand kilometers from Moscow. For a comparison of distances, both New York and Khabarovsk are eight time zones away from Moscow, but of course in opposite directions. I found it strange to take a nine-hour flight and still be in the same country; I found it equally strange to be in Russia yet only a commuter-plane distance from Japan or Korea and looking out my hotel window at Chinese mountains across the beautiful Amur River.

The Russian Far East was colonized by Russia in the second half of the nineteenth century after Russia and China signed agreements that divided the area into spheres of influence in 1858. Much as in North America colonization, native peoples in the region became increasingly marginalized in their own land in the Russian Far East and relegated to a depressed minority status. At the Museum of Far East History, I was especially impressed by two eerie comparisons that leaped to mind. First, the native art was remarkably similar to the stone carvings of Canadian Inuit (Eskimo) and to the swirling bird images of North American Indians. Second, the museum artifacts and displays were arranged and explained in precisely the same way that local museums chronicled the saga of the white pioneers of the North American West. The Russian Far East was this country's version of the American/Canadian West.

Okay—back to that little word. The first day of the conference was divided into two halves. In the morning, the entire assemblage—about two hundred professors, cultural workers, and government representatives—gathered in one meeting to hear four plenary addresses, and in the afternoon, smaller groups met to give and discuss papers in three simultaneous academic sessions. I gave one of the morning plenary talks because I was Mr. Fulbright Sivachev and I was pleased to feel that I did not disgrace myself, or if I did, people were too polite to say so or throw fruit. I did notice that each of us got just about the same applause, which suggests no one listened to any of us.

But, after this was over, a wonderful woman named Victoria Romanova (could a name be more royal?) told me that I was expected at a special dinner in the city's plushest hotel. Now, I must back up a bit and tell you something of Professor Romanova. She is the vice rector (vice president) of Khabarovsk University and had been asked the previous day by the government to show two of us visitors around the city. She later told me that she considered this an imposition and pain but felt duty-bound to do it. She brought along Elena, another professor who was a close friend, and the four of us—two male visitors and two local women—spent three hours together visiting some sites. Victoria is an accomplished Russian historian, charming, wonderfully cute, important, and somewhere between forty-five and fifty-five. Okay, you see my thinking now. I behaved, of course, but I did think that we had a certain attraction for each other, and when she left for a washroom break, Elena told me that Victoria was recently divorced. I thought that Victoria must have wanted me to know that, and my hunch seemed borne out by Elena taking the other professor to a museum and Victoria suggesting that she and I instead walk along the river. To make a long story longer, therefore, Victoria and I discovered that we did indeed like each other. This, be assured, is the wildest part of my story and nothing untoward happened (alas).

But – back to dinner – which is lunch by our standards since it was to be served at half past noon. Victoria took me to an elegant but small dining room in the plush hotel and we sat at a table for fourteen people: the four plenary speakers from the morning, Victoria and two people from the university, and assorted other representatives from national and state governments and cultural organizations. I was the only American, but a German was also present. He and I were each to have an interpreter, but Victoria had agreed to be mine. The table groaned under food and also under wine and vodka bottles. Remember, it was the middle of the day. About five minutes into stuffing ourselves, one of our number jumped up – the other visiting professor on my outing with Victoria and Elena the day before, and himself a plenary session speaker. He gave a long, impassioned and well-received toast as we all stood – Victoria translated for me – and then we all clinked vodka glasses and no one missed another of the other thirteen, and chugged down the vodka, which was brown, not clear white, and was a known local brand.

The waiters sprang to action before we sat down and when our drained glasses hit the table, they were immediately filled. A toast was nice, I thought. Russians are good hosts. About three more minutes into the jellied salmon, a government guy jumped up and, of course, we all did. He, too, gave a long toast, again with the thirteen clinks and the empty vodka glass. When the third guy jumped up less than five minutes later, I saw the writing on the wall and was pleased to think that there were only fourteen of us. And so it went – huge amounts of food and fourteen toasts and, of course, I gave mine, which Victoria translated.

When lunch was over, I was not reeling or slurring but I was aware of the vodka sousing that I had just endured. (Enjoyed?) Somehow I survived two more hours of academic papers and got back to the hotel about 5:00. Victoria – who does not drive but as vice rector has a car and driver – dropped me off and said that I was invited to a special reception in the hotel private dining hall at 7:00. We agreed to meet there. And here is where the language problem occurred – with one innocuous (or so I thought) little word: *reception.*

I was darn tired and would like to have taken a nap, but I knew that if I did so I was done for and would see neither reception nor Victoria that night. Not just the vodka strained my stamina; I was operating eight time zones out of whack with a jet lag and having missed a night's sleep a day earlier due to an overnight flight. Still, I am a tough guy, so I checked e-mail and sat down in my boxer shorts at 6:00 to watch the television news. I thought an hour of CNN International would rejuvenate me and I would get dressed about 7 and wander into the reception about 7:30. Who wants to be the first person to show up for a reception?

At 7:00, I was brushing my teeth and still in my skivvies when the phone rang. It was Victoria. "Where are you, everyone is waiting? Is anything wrong?"

Being a cool dude, I do not panic, but I am a bit surprised. I told her that I was coming and should be there by 7:30 and I asked her if she was really looking forward so much to seeing me.

Victoria back to me: "You must get down here, right now" – I thought that I heard the silent noun "jackass" in her command but I may have been mistaken – "nothing can start until you get here."

Ever the cool dude, I still don't panic, but I do catch my breath. "Okay," I tell her, "I'll be there in five minutes," and I was. I have never dressed as quickly or badly in my life, and when I cleared the elevator on the first floor, two men were waiting and practically picked me up and ran me to the private dining room, where I encountered a strange scene.

What do we mean by "reception" in New Hampshire, Manitoba or Texas? To us, a reception is a sort of drop-in, drop-out, come and go at your leisure cocktail party where a person circulates, makes mindless small talk, drinks a beer or wine in one hand, munches on snacks, and tries not to be caught by the biggest bore in the room or to be the biggest bore that everyone tries to avoid. An American or Canadian reception is usually casual, and any ceremony is usually perfunctory and consists of thanking hosts or presenting an award or telling the guests to enjoy themselves.

As I found out, Russian "receptions" may be different or the choosing of the word "reception" to characterize this evening may have been inappropriate. The room had a huge table laden with food, places set on all four sides of the table, and no chairs. About forty or fifty people were standing on the four sides of the table which resembled a food mountain, and no one had touched a morsel until I walked (was thrown? stumbled?) in. Victoria stood facing the door and next to her was the only empty place at the table. I assumed my position and the festivities began. I could see what was coming – toasts and more toasts and yet more toasts. Even I, the biggest social oaf in Russia, knew of course that not everyone would give a toast – forty glasses of vodka would be beyond even Russians – even Far East, hardy pioneer Russians. Nor could we clink all other thirty-nine glasses – those of immediate neighbors had to do. The toasts were longer and much more elaborate than at lunch and Victoria translated them for me.

So, eight time zones out of joint, missing a night's sleep, recovering from a degenerate lunch, trying to smile and clink my way out of explaining my rude lateness, and much smitten with Victoria, I started to get the rhythm of the whole dang thing – as my Texas friends might say – and the vodka really made the toasts lyrical. Imagine my horror, however, when on about the sixth or seventh go-round – counting was becoming difficult – the presiding officer brought portable microphones to Victoria and me and said that I must make a toast. Victoria introduced me as the Fulbright Chair from Moscow and then said to me that she would translate for me but that I should speak slowly and clearly. Now Victoria speaks perfect English but she is not a professional translator and was also a bit out of practice. Many times during our conversations, I had to repeat or rephrase things.

Okay, now the late American who made every hungry (and thirsty) person wait for ten long minutes is given a chance to redeem himself. He must get his wits together but he has had no chance to prepare. And he must speak slowly – always tough for this American. And he must speak clearly, despite the vodka assaulting his sleepless body. He can do it – or he thinks he can. I still do not panic but only by summoning up all the resistance possible. I started my toast with a statement about New York,

Toronto, Moscow, London, Paris, and Tokyo that said people in these cities assume that they are the ultimate expression of their respective cultures. My plan was to go on to say that in reality, it is the Winnipegs and Lubbocks and Khabarovsks and the thousands of small cities and villages that are the real repositories of a nation's spirit and culture. And then go on from there to wax on about my newly discovered love for the Russian Far East. It would have worked – I know it would have. But, after I pause midway, waiting for Victoria's translation, I wait and wait and hear nothing from behind me where she stands. Then I hear, "Bruce, I don't understand what you are saying."

Now is the time. I panic – a real genuine panic. What to do? Fake a heart attack? Start a food fight? Say, "God bless the Red Sox"? (I did think of that.) I did none of the foregoing but regrouped pathetically and gave the most vacuous toast of the night. I honestly forget what I said but it was something like, "To your health and to Khabarovsk." I am sure that the common sentiment was: *We waited ten long minutes without drinking and that's what we get?*

What to do? It was not my fault, and if I had only known that, in this case, the word "reception" really meant "very formal boozing and toasting time; please be punctual and clever," I would have done a great job.

WHAT DID I LEARN? Translation is an inexact science and Russians – even academics – are a boisterous lot.

DO NOT LEAVE THE WINDOW OPEN

Many little legacies of the Soviet cradle-to-grave welfare state linger and have an uneven effect on what is otherwise one of the world's most aggressive market economies. Apartment heating is one of these. Russia and Moscow are cold places and the Soviet government guaranteed heat to all people virtually free of charge. The Russian government still does. Buildings are heated by the government and individual apartment dwellers whether renters or owners have no thermostat to set or bill to pay. The heat just comes and is ample – often too ample, and my flat is occasionally so hot that it is almost unlivable. What to do? I asked friends and they tell me to open a small window even in the dead of winter. "Doesn't this waste a lot of energy?" They shrug, so I open.

Probably the heating arrangements are controlled by a computer some-where, because if the weather suddenly spikes to an extreme, the overheat-ing problem becomes acute as the computer struggles to change as rapidly as the thermometer. In early April, the temperature went from about $-8°$ to $+8°$C, and I was living in a sauna. Opening the little window did not do the job, so I took the plunge and opened a large one that is about four meters high. I did not like wasting all that heating energy, but the air felt wonder-ful. I was typing away at this very keyboard and feeling very comfortable when suddenly all Hell broke loose. Well perhaps "all Hell" is a bit strong; probably during the war when the Nazis suddenly dropped bombs on an apartment block, that sort of activity would be more deserving of the description. But barring a ton or two of TNT on your head, a large bird out of nowhere will come darn close to inspiring an "all Hell" feeling. A big black uninvited something flew in the window and was just as displeased to be in my apartment as I was to have it. It looked like a crow but did not make the *"caw, caw"* distinctive crow sound, unless crows caw differently in Russ-ian from in English. It made a screeching noise, however, and it made it a lot as the poor thing careened about my tiny place, smacking into walls and doors and everything. I made a screeching noise, too.

After nearly suffering a heart attack from the frightening surprise, I made an instant tactical decision which I knew brought with it the possibility of greater disaster: I opened all the windows, fully aware that this raven's flock-mates might join the party before he left. I grabbed a broom and chased him – I have decided it was a boy-bird because he was so rude – and miracle of miracles, he flew out within ten seconds. The grand opening was followed quickly by a grand closing, and I will restrict myself to the little window in the future. He could fly through the little space, but he would have to want to come in for a visit, and my guess is that the bird was just as surprised and unhappy as I was when he flew into the open space of the big window.

WHAT DID I LEARN? Clever people can always blame someone else for their mistakes. In Winnipeg, I had small birds fly down my fireplace three or four times over a twenty-year period, but never the avian equivalent of a Boeing 747. I hold the Communists fully accountable for this terrifying experience. If they had not wanted everyone in Russia to be warm, I would never have had to suffer as I did.

MY BATTLE WITH MOSCOW'S GREATEST CLERK

As you know from earlier scribbles, I do not have an unduly high opinion of Moscow's clerks but, nevertheless, I have always believed that given enough time and repeated contact, I can – through smiles, friendly hellos, tips of the hat, little salutes – force even the most committed sourpuss on the planet into a grudging acknowledgment of humanity. Therefore, I have done battle throughout my stay on behalf of the Daniels principle of excessive friendliness, and deliberately cultivated personal relationships with people in my neighborhood, most of whom I cannot talk to in a language they understand. To wit: two souvenir-stand hawkers on the Arbat and I have become pals through two separate schticks. One always said "Souvenirs, nearly free," as I walked by and I would laugh and say, "free, I want free." Gradually, this became our greeting – every bit as vacuous as two guys in Winnipeg or Lubbock saying "cold day" or " too hot" each morning in passing. "Still nearly free," he always says, and I counter with, "I want free," and we both laugh.

The other souvenir guy and I just always shake hands. I started it, but he likes it, and we each say something mutually unintelligible after every handshake, whereby we have built a bonded relationship that I value. And so it goes; the main doorman at the Golden Ring Hotel where I pick up my morning copy of *The Moscow Times* and I exchange incomprehensible but warm greetings every morning; he holds the door for me and I give him a pat on the shoulder for thanks; the secondary doorman and I always exchange tips of the hat. A bank guard that I walk by points to my head if I am not wearing a hat and admonishes me with a grin even though I do not understand his specific words; in warm weather I do not need a hat, of course, but by then we have a fast friendship. An eighteen-year-old girl who sells snacks in a kiosk always says "you're welcome" loudly in response to my *"spaceba"* ("thank you" in Russian) and we both exhaust one-fourth of our vocabulary. I bribed my way to favorite-customer status by excessive tipping – 15 percent as opposed to the usual nothing most customers give – in a little bistro on the Arbat where I often stop. Waiters and waitresses greet me warmly, give me a seat at the window if it is cold and on the patio if it is warm, and know just what beer to bring me.

And so it goes – one small smile for man, one small step for humanity. And with each little social conquest, I crossed the line from public coldness to personal warmth. It felt good. But one clerk eluded my charm (for lack of a better word to describe my frontal assault of friendliness) for three full months and stands as a monument to the non-involvement school of human relations. Steely, determined, and utterly un-tempted ever to bend her rigid standards, she should be a heroine to the clerk's union. Yet a little detail in the post-battle analysis suggests that the story had an even greater complexity than I had imagined.

Ms. Stone Clerk worked in the little grocery store nearest me where I stopped virtually every day to buy two one-liter bottles of purified water for drinking. Moscow water is safe to drink but it tastes skunky, so most people buy water for drinking and cooking, as do I. The bottles are somewhat heavy so I buy them in the store that will require me to carry them the least distance home. Every time I entered the store, I went to the cooler and got the bottles myself; they cost twenty rubles each, and usually I had the correct change needed of forty rubles. I would put the two bottles in front of Ms. Stone Clerk and give her the forty rubles along with my usual smile and pathetic English blather. All Russians – probably all people – know that "Hi" is a greeting and that a smile is a greeting, too. Never once did Ms. Stone Clerk ever show the slightest flicker of recognition. Day after day, week after week, water bottle after water bottle; never did any emotion cross her face other than a stony – I mean an absolute stony – stare. Every time I entered that store, it appeared to be the first time that I had ever been seen. But this was not what elevated Ms. Stone Clerk above all others. No, what raised Ms. Stone Clerk to the exalted rank of greatness was the daily bagging routine we went through.

Two one-liter bottles are too unwieldy to carry by themselves and I would always ask her for a bag. This language, of course, is more complicated than saying "hi," and I realized that at first she did not know what I was saying. But the plastic bags were directly next to her and I pointed to them. The first time I did this, she looked slowly at the pile of bags and then – with incredible deliberation – picked up a bag and slowly handed it to me. Scorn showed everywhere in the act. Contempt was too mild a term – only scorn will do for this wonderfully understated but overwhelming theatric that would have made Katharine Hepburn envious. But here is the beauty of this unparalleled artist's commitment to her craft: every single day that I bought water, the same drama played out. I must have bought water from this clerk at least fifty times and never once did she deviate from the same routine. I thought that perhaps she was starting a schtick with me as her way of creating a bond. If so, she gave no sign of anything – never a word, never a smile nor shrug, and certainly never a bag without the same prompting and then the slow, contemptuous reach. Ms. Stone Clerk displayed little greater warmth with other customers, but clearly did her job well aside from the deep-freeze zone she created by the force of her personal iciness.

But I kept thinking, how long can she keep this up? Will she ever give me a bag without being asked? As weeks stretched into months, I realized that Ms. Stone Clerk never took a day off. Day after day from 9 a.m. to 9 p.m. she stood behind the same counter and looked sullen – completely refusing unnecessary conversation with all comers. And then one day she was gone and I never saw her again. Maybe her dream job in customer relations came through and she is now staring from behind a better counter, or a complaint desk, or a gun. Her replacement seems vacuously sunny and garrulous – not really but by contrast – but lacks her predecessor's memorable character. But get this: I again had to point to the pile of bags; Ms. Sunshine immediately gave me one and then said, "three rubles." She charged me three rubles for the bag and now when I go to the store, Ms. Sunshine gets the bag out for me without my asking, but always charges me the same extra three rubles.

WHAT DID I LEARN? I have learned a little ecological lesson. Now I bring a crumpled-up plastic bag with me in order to save the three-ruble charge. And I wonder why Ms. Stone Clerk never charged me for the bags. I wonder if she were fired because other customers complained that she was simply too, too hostile. Most of all, I wonder if she will survive as a clerk as Russia evolves, for I know she will not change.

THE TURKEY DROP

About two months before I came to Russia, the U.S. Embassy in Moscow put me on a list of people who receive a monthly report on crimes against Americans in Russia. One of the most recent and most frequent is the "turkey drop" in which the honesty of foreign tourists is used against them. Here's how it goes. The foreigner – the turkey – is walking in a crowded area when someone brushes by him (turkeys are usually men, but not always) and apparently unintentionally drops a large wad of cash in a money clip. The turkey bends down and picks up the wad and yells, "Sir, sir, you dropped your life's savings." The turkey is now ready to be plucked. A third party from behind grabs him and yells, "thief, thief" or the equivalent in a language that no turkey can understand, and the alleged victim – the wad dropper – now turns around to come back and join the screaming. Usually the good Samaritan-accomplice and the dropper do a great deal of shoving of the turkey who, understandably if not forewarned, still thinks he is the victim of a misunderstanding. By all accounts, however, the experience is terrifying.

On sophisticated turkey drops, two policemen also enter the scene. There is no place that one can walk in Moscow and not have policemen within sight. Like nuns, they always travel in twos, and they are everywhere. This would be reassuring if they were honest, *but they are not.* (More on this below). The police come over and talk to the Samaritan, the wad-dropper, and the turkey, but of course, of these five people, four speak Russian and one speaks English and four are in a conspiracy and one is just beginning to understand that he is a turkey. From wild gestures and a little English here and there, the turkey comes to understand that he is accused of stealing the wad and, despite the wad's presence, some of it is missing – probably the turkey had an accomplice, he is told. Such is the righteous indignation of the alleged victim and the Good Samaritan, that the police must restrain them from attacking the turkey. Charges must be preferred unless the money is restored. Very often, the turkey has now been moved to a police car – perhaps for his own protection – and is sitting in the back seat with hands cuffed.

It all sounds horribly scary. At a recent security meeting that I was asked to attend at the embassy, the assigned officer explained it in person and said it was now epidemic and if one did not know about it – and most tourists without an official government connection do not know about it – the crime is remarkably effective in getting the turkey to give all the money he has with him just to get out of the situation. The security officer told us that if we were here very long, we would be a targeted turkey at some point and the defense was to spin to the side and walk as fast as one can directly away from the dropped wad. Do not look at it, do not look around, do not talk to anyone – spin sideways and do not do a complete turnaround, because the accomplice is probably behind you – and then walk quickly away but do not run. This has two effects: first it gets you away from the scene, and second, it alerts the conspiracy to the fact that you know exactly what is going on: You know a turkey drop when you see one.

Well, one day in March I was walking out of Red Square when a guy brushed by me, and a wad of cash dropped out of his pocket. I spun to my left immediately and walked away and heard a voice behind me say, "Mister, look at that money." I did not turn to see who said this; I did not stop for one hundred meters and when I did, there was no sign of any conspirators. They were off to get an unsuspecting turkey who had not been warned, and I was a free and darn lucky bird.

WHAT DID I LEARN? I am usually skeptical about a lot of the junk we get from governments about matters like this, but if I had not known about the turkey drop, I would have bent down, picked up the wad, called out to the dropper, and been in big trouble. Sometimes it pays to listen to people with experience.

And now a little more on crime. Once again, I tend to skepticism about stories of corruption, but it is safe to say that the Moscow police are rotten throughout. All Russians say this and, as it turns out, all police say this, too. Let me illustrate this with three separate stories of police corruption reported in the *Moscow Times*.

STORY ONE. A reporter interviewed members of Moscow's drug police squads. According to the reporter, every single cop – without exception – said that all police (including themselves) engage in some corruption. The distinction they made between honest and dishonest cops is an old one that late nineteenth-century American urban politicians made between good graft and bad graft. Somehow among the ranks, the police know which cops cross the line from acceptable forms of bribery to unacceptable ones. The story reported that senior police were paid about 8,000 rubles a month (a little less than $300 US) and new recruits about half of that. No one can survive and raise a family and have a car on that money, one spokesperson said. And yet all police do have cars: the difference between taking good graft and bad graft is between those who drive Ladas and those who drive Mercedes, he explained.

STORY TWO. A traffic cop was shot dead after he stopped a car driving in central Moscow. Three men ran from the scene and two of them, according to the story as first reported, were masquerading as police officers. They were believed to have been extorting payoffs from motorists on trumped-up charges. Not quite the whole story, it turned out. Several days later the paper reported that the two assailants in police uniform were, indeed, harassing motorists, but they were not masquerading as police; they were off-duty policemen who had car-jacked the car of the third man, who had no money to pay them. He miraculously escaped with his life and identified the policemen who had murdered their fellow officer.

STORY THREE. This story extends beyond police corruption. A survey of international companies and executives with long experience in Moscow, reported that 86 percent of them said that corruption at all levels in Russian government and law enforcement was the most serious problem they faced when doing business in Russia.

I was the target of two unsuccessful crimes in my first two months in Russia – the police shakedown and the turkey drop. It did not make me feel very secure. Ed Roslof, the director of academic exchanges in Russia, is an American but he speaks fluent Russian and has spent more than a decade of his life here doing research and as an administrator. He has been here a little more than two years on this current assignment and, as savvy as Ed is, during these two years he has been violently mugged as he entered his own apartment and pick-pocketed on the metro.

I took some other advice from the security officers at the Embassy. I carried nothing in my wallet but money – no driver's license, no credit or ATM cards. If I was going to charge something or get cash, I put the one necessary card in my wallet for that occasion only. So, if I got separated from my wallet, I would lose only the relatively small amount of cash that I was carrying. A bigger fear was losing a passport, visa, or migration card, because foreigners must have these documents with them at all times and they are hot items on the black market.

STORY FOUR. Saddest of all: Conflict of interest at Moscow State.

My own school corrupt? Corruption at the finest university in the country? Say it ain't so.

The word "corruption" overstates the case. The problem is somewhat less than scandalous but more than unseemly. Additionally, the nature of the problem is known to all students and faculty. Getting into Moscow State is extraordinarily difficult, but depends primarily on doing well on the University's own admission exam. Fair enough. Prospective students, or more properly the student's parents, usually hire tutors who help them prepare for these exams. Again, fair enough. Many Moscow State professors take part-time jobs tutoring future students for these exams. Perhaps fair enough, but a whiff of something fishy is in the air. The professors conduct the admission exams, all of which are oral and very subjective. Thus the highly paid tutors examine their own clients. Remember, students apply directly to departments as part of their admission process, so tutors are almost always guaranteed to evaluate exams of students by whom they have been paid large sums of money to help prepare. We now detect not so much the stench of corruption, but still the unpleasant odor of conflict of interest.

Having written all the above, which makes Moscow sound like Chicago circa 1928, I should conclude by saying that I survived my sojourn completely unscathed by serious crime. I fended off the inept police shakedown, I sidestepped the Turkey Drop, and I neither took nor offered any bribes to students. One afternoon I did hear gunshots and screeching tires outside of my flat; the police arrived a few minutes later but I saw no bodies or blood and I assume that a traffic altercation had lead to a scary scene that produced more noise than real violence. My only loss to crime was a Texas Tech baseball hat that some wretch pilfered from my restaurant chair while I went to the bathroom. It may give him limited utility, for I told sixty students in my lecture that if they saw anyone in Moscow wearing a TTU cap that they should thump the bugger as either a thief or a receiver of stolen goods. On the crime ledger, I may actually appear on the wrong side of the balance sheet. I often stopped in a hotel bar near my flat and became friendly with the waiters who would occasionally give me a free unsolicited second beer when I finished my first. I believe that they sometimes put these freebees on the bills of large groups of loud tourists who annoyed them and had no idea how many beers they had consumed.

Most importantly, however, despite all the appropriate warnings, not once did I feel threatened on the street. I never held my breath walking by a bunch of street thugs or had to avert a fight or had a feeling of being stalked. No one in a coffee shop or bar ever said something that I took to be challenging. Even more amazingly, in hundreds of shopping transactions in local markets, I did not experience any attempt to shortchange me even though I would have been a ready mark for any such effort. Whether buying tomatoes or chicken thighs from local farmers with whom I could not exchange more than smiles, I feel that I was always treated honestly. This is really quite extraordinary and suggests something of the quiet dignity with which the new humble, rural capitalists conduct their market lives, and of the kindness that this poor mute professor experienced as he gestured his way through Russian life.

CHAPTER FIVE

Russian Customs
Furs, Hats, Tipping, and Valentine's Day

If visitors want to be well received, they should learn the local rhythms by which most people live. Russian customs for most of the twentieth century combined conservative village tradition and Communist-mandated reform into an odd amalgam that seemed alternately behind and ahead of the rest of western Europe and North America. This is not surprising; cultures almost always have deeply embedded idiosyncrasies that had economic, social, or climate-related origins, and pre-Revolutionary Russia had lagged behind the West in modernizing. Many rural mores survived unscathed throughout the Soviet era alongside explicit changes that the Communist Party thought appropriate for a worker's utopia. Both village ethos and Communist innovation persist in the new Russia, but both are colliding with the subversive forces of urbane globalism.

Old habits die hard. In a remarkably agrarian dietary habit, Russians eat dinner in the middle of the day and call the evening meal the equivalent of supper, much as North American farmers once did but seldom do now. Canadian and American farmers formerly ate their biggest meal at noon because they had been up since 5 a.m. milking and working hard all morning. With good reason they were hungry by the middle of the day. They ate a small meal, supper, at 6 or 7 p.m. because they tumbled into bed soon after. Moscow's food clock today is similar to yesterday's farmers in the West but for almost opposite reasons. Perhaps historically they were the same, but not now. Moscow people get up much later – it is regarded as impolite to call a home before 10 a.m. – and they go to bed much later – you may call up until 11 p.m. without being rude. Instead of business offices opening at 8 or 8:30 a.m. as they do in North America, Moscow offices sometimes open at 9:30 a.m. but more usually at 10:00. They close correspondingly later. When I say to a Muscovite that I will call on the phone, he or she – undoubtedly conditioned by a few bad experiences – will often say, "yes, but not too early." "Those damn Americans" must be the underlying thought.

So, Russians eat like farmers but sleep like night owls. Here is the clock my Moscow colleagues live by:

ARISE: 8:30 to 9 a.m.

BREAKFAST: 9:30 a.m.; the size of breakfast varies but tends toward the substantial; porridge is very popular in winter in most households.

MOSCOW RUSH HOURS FOR METRO: 9:30 to 11 a.m.; 6:30 to 8:30 p.m.

NORMAL BUSINESS HOURS: 10 a.m. to 7 p.m.

PREFERRED AND USUAL CLASS HOURS: 11 a.m. to 6 p.m. Professors go to the university only for classes or meetings: they have no offices and do not work there. Students similarly are usually there just for classes.

DINNER: 2 to 4 p.m., a big meal if possible, almost always with meat; this can be difficult for families and students but it is the goal. Beer and/or vodka are often served and especially if a guest is present.

SUPPER: 8:30 to 9:30 p.m., not the light meal of North American farmers but a substantial second big meal with a main meat dish.

BEDTIME: Midnight to 1 a.m.

Naming patterns also cling to an older tradition than in the West and even in ultramodern Moscow are uniformly based on patriarchy. Thus my first name would be given to any of my children as a middle name, with a suffix added to it meaning "son of" which is "-ivich" or "daughter of" which is "-ovna." Girls also add an "a" to the end of their surname to show that they are, indeed, female. "Bruce" is not a Russian name so there is no exact equivalent, but most people agree that in forming my daughters' names, the last "e" would probably be dropped so that two vowels would not appear together. Slavic languages do not mind having consonants tripping over each other but tend to be less vowel-friendly.

Thus, my daughter's names would most likely be:

Elizabeth Daniels: Yelizaveta Brucovna Danielsa;
Abigail Daniels: Abigaila Brucovna Danielsa;
Nora Daniels: Nora Brucovna Danielsa.

I would be Bruce Howardivich Daniels because I am the son of Howard Daniels.

My Moscow friends, and indeed most Russians, commonly refer to each other by their first and second names when speaking to a third party: thus one of my daughter's friends, when talking to another about her, would likely use the equivalent of "Elizabeth, daughter of Bruce" to identify her instead of "Elizabeth Daniels."

President Vladimir Putin's father was also named "Vladimir" so newspaper stories trying to effect an intimacy about him – usually sarcastically – refer to him as "Vladimir Vladimirivich" which is, of course, "Vladimir, son of Vladimir."

These are ancient naming customs.

Muscovites have more traditional clothes-wearing habits than we do in the West. They wear hats in the winter even on relatively warm days. The winter reminds me much of Boston weather – far warmer than Winnipeg – yet even on days when the temperature has been above 0°C (32°F) it is almost impossible to see anyone without a hat.

However, hat culture shows some signs of undergoing modernization. In the United States, President John Kennedy is alleged to have killed the hat industry when he showed up bareheaded to take the oath of office on a winter day in 1961. In the 1950s, well-dressed American and Soviet men had uniformly worn the same Fedora hats. After JFK, men forswore hats unless absolutely required by weather, except of course for ball caps, which North American men started wearing on all occasions about twenty years ago. I am not sure if JFK or someone or something else occasioned the parallel decline in hat wearing for American women.

In Moscow, today, the poor *ushanka* may be sharing the Fedora's fate. What is the *ushanka*? You do know it – you just do not know its name. The *ushanka* is that stereotypical Russian hat – the big furry one that stands high on the wearer's head and has earflaps that can be pulled down if needed. The hat appears so ubiquitously in pictures of Muscovites trudging through snow and cold that it is known everywhere in the world as "the Russian hat," but the name used here is *ushanka*. When I told a friend I was coming to Moscow he asked, "will you buy one of those hats?" I replied, "No, I already own one" (which I had bought as a tourist).

When I first arrived, I saw *ushankas* aplenty, and every souvenir-stand operator tried to sell me one as I walked by – they called them "Russian hats." "Hey, mister, buy a Russian hat cheap – real fur." I assumed therefore that the *ushanka* – this international winter symbol of Soviet manhood – was in no danger of being, like the Communist Party, an artifact of a bygone era. And why should it? The hat is darn functional. But, after becoming a bit more discerning in my observation, I noticed that *ushanka* wearers invariably had hair color – gray – to match their hats or, alternately, *ushanka* wearers looked like tourists. So, I turned to my students – the fount of all popular-culture knowledge – to enlighten me. And here is the story:

The *ushanka* is a generation marker that old men hold onto proudly – but younger, more hip guys would rather be caught wearing a red brassiere and skimpy panties while talking on a cell phone than be caught with a dead wolf on their head. The *ushanka* is worn by three groups of people: old men, foreign tourists, and absolute nerds. The *ushanka* has become the Russian equivalent to the North American plastic pen holder that fits in a man's shirt pocket and is a registered, certifiable, universally acknowledged trademark of unquestionable dorkhood. When the women in my classes were asked if they would date a guy wearing an *ushanka*, they all rolled their eyes and giggled.

So tourists buy *ushankas* to be Russian – and in doing so they stamp themselves either as tourists or as Russian nerds. I, by the way, did not bring my *ushanka* to Russia with me, but if I did, I am of such an age that I would offer the choice to passersby of being either a tourist or a proud, old Soviet soldier. I would be too old to be thought of as a nerd. Russian women also wear winter hats, but no single style dominates.

But there is more to the modern anthropology of Moscow hat wearing. On the first very warm day of spring, I sat in a window seat on the Arbat sipping tea – probably one-fourth of my waking Moscow hours could be described thusly – and noticed the new warm-weather choice of hats. Middle-aged and old men – yesterday's *ushanka* wearers – traded their pieces of wolf in for those little caps where the top is fastened to a tiny brim with one button. I always think of these hats as English, perhaps because the cartoon character Andy Capp habitually wore one, but they are ubiquitous here in Moscow, although only with men more than forty years old. In size, the Russian hat and the English cap could not be more opposite. But now the symbolism loses all ambiguity. Since tourists do not wear the English caps, there is no defense against the nerd charge if you are twenty-one and caught wearing one. Young men either discard their hats to embrace bareheaded abandon after a long winter of disheveled hat-hair, or they wear baseball caps as do the young guys in North America. Hat culture is beginning to go global in Moscow.

One clothing custom clearly flies in the face of popular or politically correct trends. The international campaign to stop the wearing of animal furs has failed to get its message heard in Russia. Most well-dressed Moscow women have fur coats and fur hats. Every woman colleague of mine at the university without exception wears a fur coat, including several who are labor and farmer-movement historians and thus inclined towards a radical persuasion of intellectual life. At least half of my women students wear them and I am sure that the rest would too, if furs were not so expensive. I am not much of a judge of fur quality, but most of the ones I see look tasteful – if wearing fur can be tasteful today – and are not gaudy. When I asked a colleague about the coats, she replied simply, "they are warm." Men do not wear fur coats, but most wear fur hats.

What to do with your fur coat at the ballet? Coat checking is a mania in all public places. As soon as a customer enters a restaurant, a greeter instructs him or her where to go to check the coat. Draping a coat across your dinner chair, as is done so much in North America, is discouraged by frowns. At concert halls and theaters, coat checking is a science. *Give me your coat.* Over a dozen clerks take coats and one must redeem a coat with the same clerk who took it because they each will handle a specific range of numbers. If your coat does not have an inside loop to aid in the hanging, clerks are displeased and will show it.

I usually tip the clerk at the coat-check booth but most Russians do not. Tipping is politically controversial in Moscow. For most North Americans, a tip to a waitperson is obligatory – bad service gets 10 percent and you feel guilty, good service gets 20 percent and you feel like a philanthropist, and the average is 15 percent, which is like a tax but not legally enforceable. In Russia, the world of tipping is different and is very much connected to history. Unlike France and many European countries where the 15 percent is literally added into the bill and hence the tip is legally unavoidable, in Russia it is not. But customers are told that the tip is included because wait people are paid a good wage. Still, that is not a tip. But here is where the Soviet past intrudes. Almost all people who ideologically supported the principles of Soviet Communism are against tipping because they argue that it suggests that waitpersons are servants and hence, the concept of tipping is demeaning to the person who receives the tip. Waitpersons are fellow citizens, not subordinates at the diner's beck and call. I am told by nearly everyone that people over the age of fifty seldom tip because of this ideological sense of what the act implies. I believe them, and further I believe that it is not a mask for being cheap, but an honest sense that tipping makes the wait staff beggars of sorts, or people forced to grovel, and that this is offensive. Today many young wait staff, I am sure, would say, *Spare me the ideology and leave me a few rubles.* And despite the fact that their parents do not, most young Russians do indeed leave tips, although usually less than the western world's 15 percent.

But here is the kicker in terms of social class. My students all agreed that waiting on tables should not make a server into a servant; in this sense, my students were true democrats. But when I asked if any of them had ever waited on tables to make a little extra spending money, they all gave me a blank — *of course not* — look. They were university students at Moscow State and future leaders, not waiters and waitresses. The blank stares grew more wide-eyed when I told them that I had been a busboy, waiter, and bartender at various times in my life and was mighty pleased to get every tip I could. In Winnipeg and Lubbock, I cannot walk into a restaurant without bumping into a university student who will serve me a beer or hot dog. That is not the case in Moscow, where I would be unlikely ever to be waited on by a university student.

And talking as we were about the plight of the *ushanka* and of small sums of money, I would like you to consider the plight of the poor little kopec. For years Canadians and the English have wondered why the United States continues to print one-dollar bills when their value has been so debased by inflation. The pound has been a coin for at least a quarter century and the Canadian Loonie replaced the one-dollar bill sometime in the early 1980s. Americans respond invariably with a nonsensical answer:

It was tried once – the Susan B. Anthony dollar coin – and the public would not accept it. The logic here has two problems: first, why will Americans not accept a coin when everyone else in the world will? And second, of course no one liked the Susan B. Anthony dollar because it was nearly identical to the quarter and confused everyone – it was poorly designed. The problem should have been not with the concept of a dollar coin, but with that specific dopey coin design.

Having unburdened myself about the one-dollar bill, let me turn to the poor little American and Canadian penny. Long ago, before my time, the penny was a serious coin. Even in my childhood, a kid could save a mere five pennies and get a whole candy bar. For a penny, gum machines gave you a good chew. Some charities allegedly gathered enough spare pennies to benefit humankind. But pennies are now absolutely useless and an annoyance that weighs down your pockets or purse. Why are they still minted? The nickel would do just dandy all by itself at the bottom of the coin chain.

But consider the poor little kopec. For an American dollar in 2007, a person gets about twenty-seven rubles and for a Canadian dollar about twenty-four rubles. Thus, a ruble is worth a little less than four American or five Canadian pennies. The ruble is a decimal currency and is divided into one hundred kopecs; thus, a kopec is worth less than four-hundredths of an American penny and five-hundredths of a Canadian penny. And the Russian government still mints one-kopec coins. What on earth can one do with one kopec? No bills are ever tendered that knowingly charge a kopec, but when goods are sold by weight, the charge often requires a kopec or so in change. Why not round it off? I have an apartment filled with one-kopec coins. The kopec makes American and Canadian pennies look like major money. Why not get rid of it? Even the five-kopec coin seems a bit silly; one would have to save six kopec nickels to make them worth an American penny.

My point with both the American refusal to abandon the one-dollar bill (or talk honestly about why not) and the Russian refusal to stop minting one-kopec coins is that we were darn lucky to get through the Cold War without blowing the world up.

Perhaps the survival of the little kopec is in some strange way a symbol of frugality on the part of Russians and this attention to small sums of money accounts for the fact that Russians have virtually no personal debt. Americans and Canadians are swimming (or sinking) in personal debt and western Europeans are too, although to a lesser degree. Some of this personal debt is intelligently assumed, productive of a social good, and easily managed – a home mortgage is the best example of personal debt that most of us feel is usually a smart burden to assume. Loans for education or other big-ticket items like automobiles may or may not be good debt depending on the circumstances. Credit-card debt to finance excessive consumption is commonplace in western culture and is usually bad debt. But for better or worse, most members of western society have personal debts. Not so in Russia.

Before the public Soviet economy gave way to the private economy of the new Russia, virtually everyone in the country lived in government-owned housing. That was then given to them free of mortgage. Although housing is far less than sumptuous by western standards, most Russian families became outright owners of their homes free of encumbrances. This transition occurred in the mid-1990s and served that generation well, but of course young people growing up today must live either with their parents as young adults, rent flats, or buy their own homes. Apartment blocks are going up everywhere in Moscow, but to date, no practice of issuing mortgages has emerged. People must pay the full sum for their home upon purchase.

Similarly, everyone who buys a car must save the entire amount and then pay it at purchase time. And very few Russians have credit cards. Most of my professorial acquaintances do not have any credit card, as opposed to a majority of university students in the United States and Canada, who have several. Until very recently, Russian students paid no tuition for education, and most now still pay none or very little. Most live at home with their parents and there is no concept of student loans.

Hence, most Russians have little personal debt and what they have is estimated to total approximately 2 percent of the country's gross domestic product, compared to Americans and western Europeans, who respectively owe 72 percent and 51 percent of their country's GDP. If Russians do owe money, the most common debt is for children to owe money to their parents. Every thoughtful person that I talked to told me that all of the above will surely change dramatically within the next ten years and that a credit economy, which is just beginning to emerge, will soon mushroom. Housing will lead the way, and this is good; but car debt may be less good. The government has already proposed fees for all university students, and if today's consumption patterns in Moscow are a good predictive variable, look out for a society giddy with credit-card fever a decade from now.

If Russians do find themselves mired in personal debt in ten years and they are asked why, they will undoubtedly respond with the Moscow Shrug.

What types of people shrug and what types do not? New Yorkers shrug and so do the French. *Seinfeld* fans shrug, but *Mayberry RFD* devotees do not. Neither Canadians nor Texans are major shruggers although Montrealers would be an exception. People with freckles shrug less than the average, people who say "by golly" more than twice a month have never been known to shrug under any circumstances. Some types of people have shrug variants: lawyers raise their eyebrows as they shrug – probably they are taught in law school that this is a professional version that separates them from lay shruggers. Some peoples have shrug substitutes: taciturn New England Yankees say, "well …" and let their voices trail off when a shrug is needed, so that they will not be confused with a New Yorker.

Shrugs are primarily urban and urbane phenomena that are natural expressions to worldly and cynical people, or to people who like to think that they are worldly and cynical. Shrugs are given to acknowledge a gap between the ideal and real worlds. Often the shrug answers a question that seems to have no logical answer. "If he really believed adultery was wrong, why did he cheat on his wife?" A several paragraph response might begin to deal with the seemingly inexplicable, but a shrug simply says, "these things happen," based on thousands of years of history. Thus, shrugs are marvelous shorthand for amateur students of the human condition. And strangely enough, even people who themselves do not give shrugs, usually understand them. Their response often is: "oh" or more elaborately: "oh, I see," said very slowly with widening eyes.

To my amazement, I discovered that no one in the world shrugs better than Muscovites: I would bet them against Woody Allen or Jacques Chirac every time and make plenty of money. Most Muscovites shrug several times an hour during any conversation, but let me offer three examples in which they will not answer a question with words but will shrug with the equivalent language capacity of a medium-sized dissertation.

EXAMPLE 1. Stalin's Seven Sisters, those magnificent but strange gothic skyscrapers that dominate the city's architecture, were all built between 1946 and 1954. Muscovites will say matter-of-factly that for the most part, German prisoners of war supplied the grunt labor for this extraordinary enterprise that might be likened to building the Pyramids or Notre Dame. When I first heard this I replied, as any wide-eyed New Hampshire farm boy would, "But the war was over in 1945, how could they still be prisoners?" I received the most poignant shrug of my life. I received the same shrug the next time that I asked someone the same question although this time, I was not asking naïvely. What the shrug said, of course, was that although *technically* the war was over, twenty-seven million Russians had died because of someone else's aggression, and it did not seem too much of a stretch of morality to have this "someone else" commit a few resources to rebuilding the country that they had done so much to destroy.

EXAMPLE 2. My colleagues at Moscow State are brilliant, productive, clear-thinking, publishing historians. They write scholarly tomes and articles much as North American professors do, but they also write textbooks that are widely used throughout Russia and were even more widely used in the Soviet era. When I asked Moscow State friends who are of my age whether or not Communist Party officials forced them to hew to an official party line and if so, did they resent this censorship, I got the Moscow Shrug. This shrug, however, was a bit more sophisticated than the number one example above. It said, *of course they had to explain American history as an ongoing battle between capitalists and the proletariat, and, of course they may have oversimplified a bit here and there. But,* it also said, *Russian scholars basically agreed with the radical historians who taught on every large American campus and wrote about the United States from much the same point of view. Known as Progressives during the first half of the twentieth century and as the New Left in the 1960s and 1970s, these American radicals also saw American history as a ceaseless struggle between the haves and have-nots just as the textbook writers at Moscow State did.* The shrug went on to say that, *yes, sometimes we feel a little uncomfortable about having to leave out the full range of viewpoints, but this is inherently no more dishonest than American textbook writers, who would have been unlikely to explain the American Communist or Socialist political parties as idealistic institutions dedicated to the betterment of the dispossessed.*

EXAMPLE 3. I had no idea how much I–like all Americans–was obsessed by the concept of democracy. I do not think it appropriate for President Bush or other western leaders to lecture President Putin, as they all do– some more quietly than others. However, more than harboring a hope that Russia will become more democratic, I do share the Western belief that the growth of democracy here is inevitable in the long run. Whenever I men- tion any variant of the above to students, colleagues, or to any Russian who speaks English, I get a shrug. In my consultations, I have forced my students to explain this shrug, however, and since I am the professor and they are the students, they have little choice but to comply, although I know that they would rather let the facial expression stand on its own because the unspo- ken ambiguity gives it more meaning. I have done the equivalent of forcing Leonardo to tell me what he means by the smile/no-smile that he has given the Mona Lisa. I know the shrug answer, but I want to hear it articulated.

Here's how it goes. *For more than a thousand years,* they say, *Russia had no democracy under a succession of Tartars, Mongols, medieval princes, Czars, and Soviets. The people were much more interested in good bread and shelter than in John Locke and James Madison. No tradition of choosing our rulers is remotely part of any Russian's history. Democracy requires such a long apprenticeship in the polit- ical arts and we are just beginning to get the first lessons in that education at this moment. But first things first: many other things are far more important and must be attended to before the luxury of Western-style politics is fully embraced. We are used to self-serving leaders, and we expect them to put their own needs ahead of the public's, even if we do not necessarily like it. So please do not expect us to act like you in the early years of our new republic when we have such a different background and such different needs. Three steps forward, two steps back will be our political future. And we may define forward and backward steps in Russian political lan- guage, not in English.*

The shrug said it all–and probably better. Russians have a history that makes them the world's best shruggers.

THE RUSSIAN ORTHODOX CHURCH
IN EVERYDAY LIVES

During the Soviet era, the government identified the Russian Orthodox Church as an ally of the pre-Revolutionary elite forces that oppressed the people. Thus, the church as an institution suffered much, and individual church leaders suffered even more under the Soviets. Thousands were imprisoned at hard labor and treated brutally, especially in the 1920s and 1930s. During World War II, when Stalin and the Party needed to inspire the people and exhort them to great sacrifice in the war effort, religious leaders, including the patriarch of the Russian Orthodox Church (the Orthodox equivalent to Roman Catholicism's pope), were employed to help, and did so in exchange for gaining some religious and personal freedoms. Still, the church limped through the postwar era under clouds of lingering Soviet suspicion and hostility.

The Orthodox Church has emerged in the new Russia, however, as a potent social and political force. As much as most people will regard this as a good thing, a little payback from the church towards its enemies strikes me as scary. To wit: one of Moscow's important art galleries, the Sakharov Museum, mounted an art exhibit advertised as *"Caution! Religion."* The show did, indeed, display images that many religious people would find offensive in much the way that many modern artists do in North America, and of course also get denounced by churches and moralists. In the United States, often politicians try to withdraw government funding for such art, or in a few cases, have even tried to shut down the exhibit, although rarely are they successful in actually closing an exhibit that has already opened.

In Moscow, however, members of the Orthodox Church attended the exhibit and defaced and destroyed some of the individual pieces. Appropriately, the police charged the vandals with a crime against property, but inappropriately, they withdrew the prosecution after church leaders intervened on behalf of the vandals. Then, adding insult to injury, after some religious members of the Duma placed pressure on the courts, the state prosecutor instituted new charges against the museum's director, assistant director, and one artist, of inciting religious hatred. The prosecutor asked for two-year jail sentences for each of the three. If this were not terrifying enough, the verdict was "guilty" for the administrators – the artist was somehow let off the hook. The court then showed its mercy by imposing a large fine instead of jail time, but the message to the art world was clear: Do not mess with the Russian Orthodox Church.

Nor is the church's attack on an art exhibit a solitary exception. Religious zealots in the government attacked a new opera, *Rosenthal's Children,* which debuted in 2005 at the famed Bolshoi Theater. Shortly afterward, street protests in front of the Bolshoi tried unsuccessfully to stop the performances. The opera's crime? Pornography, because it portrays prostitutes in several scenes, thus defiling Russia's sacred symbol of theater and ballet. The fact that the defiling is being pointed out just at the time that the Bolshoi is getting some needed (and costly) renovations is another clear message of intimidation that some people are trying to send to the cultural world.

During my sojourn, the Church instituted a suit against the Russian importers of the American television animated comedy *The Simpsons*. The Church accused Homer, Bart, and company of subverting family values and encouraging children to disrespect their parents – probably an accurate charge – and attempted to have the Russian producers fined and the show banned. After a trial, the Church lost, but the fact that the suit was taken seriously gives some sense of the Church's new role in Russia.

How conservative is the Russian Orthodox Church? All women entering a church must cover their heads with a hat or scarf; several of my women students have told me that they find it offensive that they are not allowed to enter a church if they are wearing pants, and that the Church counsels women to be subordinate to men within family government. These restrictions and strictures are conservative, but I did not find them unduly surprising. I was shocked, however, by the following. Two of my female students took me on an outing to a museum and nearby was a brand new, modern church that has become a tourist attraction. They asked if I wished to see it and we went on what was a short side trip. At the church, one of the students, who was wearing a dress and looked eminently respectful, mysteriously declined to enter. Inside the church was beautiful and I said so to the student who remained outside. I asked her if she felt such hostility to the Orthodox Church or to Christianity that she would not enter a church building. She replied that she was a devout Christian and said shyly with much blushing that she would come back next week to see the church. I was mystified – a dumb little boy from New Hampshire again – until she then said: "it's a woman's thing."

Good gracious – my devout student friend felt uncomfortable going into the church because she was menstruating. How conservative *is* the Russian Orthodox Church? After checking with several of my colleagues, they all said the same thing: My student's attitude was "old-fashioned" (that term again), but it did not surprise them. Many women would feel the same and many would not.

After broaching the church's role with my students, the majority of whom characterize themselves as non-believers, I received an interesting assessment of its importance that seemed to command assent from most of them. According to my students, despite Soviet hostility to Christianity in all forms, throughout the Soviet era the church played a central role in the tens of thousands of small villages that constitute Russian life outside of the main cities. Small villages of twenty to thirty families would usually be arranged along one street with an Orthodox Church at the center both physically and metaphorically. Soviet opposition made only the slightest of dents in the Church's influence on the lives of Russian peasants.

Students also argued that the Orthodox Church stands as a good symbol of Russia's relationship with the rest of the Christian West. The Russian church is part of Christendom – but a very distinct part that is suspicious of its fellow Christians and believes that Catholics and Protestants alike feel superior to Russia's particular Christian tradition. The late traveling and evangelizing pope, John Paul II, wanted desperately to visit Russia, but the patriarch and leadership of the Russian Orthodox Church refused his several requests for an invitation. They regarded the pope, their fellow Christian, with much less respect than many Muslims and Jews did.

MOSCOW CELEBRATES HOLIDAYS

The re-invigorated Orthodox Church has forced Russians to rethink their traditional and Soviet holidays. Most of us tend to celebrate holidays by rote, in much the same way year after year. But holiday celebrations are of course intimately tied to the values we cherish. In North America, most of our holidays have not generated a great deal of controversy recently, although dustups over Christmas celebrations in schools have become commonplace. And Americans have created some new holidays such as Martin Luther King Jr. Day and Kwanzaa that have been associated with the civil-rights movement and black consciousness.

The people that I study historically, the Puritans, did great battle with traditional European holidays because they thought the celebrations were immoral and idolatrous. Just as reform Protestants and Catholics viewed holidays in dramatically different ways, so also do Communists and official atheists from the Soviet era and capitalists and Christians in the new Russia. What holidays to celebrate and how to celebrate them are matters of great political and public debate. It is clear to all Russians that some religious holidays have reemerged and will be celebrated on a national basis. But since the country has to be productive and people must work as much as ever, if new holidays come, what holidays must go?

As I was preparing to come to Moscow, I became aware that the Duma rushed through a bill that created a ten-day combination Christmas-New Year holiday to be celebrated in late December and early January. The Russian Orthodox calendar, like the Greek Orthodox one, designates Christmas and Easter on different days from western Christian calendars. I became aware of this long holiday because the Russian Consulate in Houston, which was issuing my visa, closed down for the ten-day period, after having been closed several days earlier for the American celebration of Christmas, and thus for nearly half a month my visa could not be processed. When the consulate re-opened, it was understandably swamped with pent-up business.

In December, everyone in Russia appeared to support the new holiday, but it was achieved by ending Constitution Day, which was less than a decade old, and taking away one day from the traditional two-day May 1 and 2 Labor Day holiday. In retrospect, however, many people think the lengthy Christmas-New Year holiday to be a mistake. Health officials reported a huge increase in deaths from alcohol abuse and alcohol-related accidents during a time when it is too cold for much outdoor recreation. Also, advocates for the poor argue that the holiday was tailored for wealthy people who could afford to pack up and travel to a warm destination, but was not suited to the needs of people living on lesser means. An extra day off at the beginning of May could be enjoyed by many more people, these reformers argue, and of course they also deplore the symbolism of adding an extra rich-person's holiday at the expense of subtracting a day that celebrated the laboring classes. So battles have been waging and will go on for the foreseeable future as Russians sort out when and why they should take a day off from work.

Things are up for grabs in this chunk of the world. Here are some curious and controversial holidays that I witnessed being celebrated.

VALENTINE'S DAY. Ten years ago, no one took any notice of Valentine's Day, but now it is big news and big business, for two reasons. First, Russians are crazy about flowers and chocolate, the two natural necessities for Valentine's celebrations; and second, in this consumer-driven society, the hucksters see a real chance to make money. Thus red hearts and Valentine's ads festooned the city for two weeks before the great day came. As usual, Moscow is ahead of the hinterlands, but beware out there in Siberia – the red heart craze is sweeping the country and will soon be coming to a kiosk near you.

DEFENDER OF THE FATHERLAND DAY (informally often called "Men's Day"). Held on February 23 to honor all those who have served in the military and thus defended the country, Defender Day honors all men, but particularly old ones. I expected big parades on Red Square but was disappointed. Crowds gathered there and elsewhere, patriotic music was played and speeches were given, but the holiday is more celebrated in homes than in the public arena. The bartender at a local hotel told me that most prostitutes will not have sex with Germans on Defender Day or on Victory Day in May.

WOMEN'S DAY. Held March 8 on a day set by the United Nations in 1975, Women's Day was first celebrated in the United States by the Socialist Party in 1909. Although American women workers created the holiday, Americans virtually ignore it at present, and I doubt that most have any idea when it comes and goes. Women's Day is widely celebrated internationally, however, and has been celebrated in Russia since 1913. It is now a national holiday that most people have free from work. But what has Women's Day become in the new Russia? I expected to see proud women marching, demanding more reform, and paying homage to past heroines – no, no, no. Women's Day here has become a combination of a second Valentine's Day and Mother's Day. Men are expected to buy large amounts of flowers for all the women in their lives – wives, girlfriends, mothers, daughters – and women are expected not to work for at least this one day in the year. Curiously, Women's Day seems to be the antithesis of a feminist holiday, and when I said this to a very successful career government worker, she replied dismissively that Russia has no feminists.

BUTTER AND PANCAKES WEEK AND DAY. To celebrate the beginning of Lent, which occurs at a different time in the Russian Orthodox Church than in the rest of Christendom, celebrations are held all of the week before Lent and end with a big celebration on the final Sunday. Traditionally, many devout Orthodox Christians went on fasts or vastly reduced diets during Lent, so they would eat like little piglets the week before. Butter and pancakes have become the treat most associated with the feasting and they are usually served outdoors because winter is starting to wane. Several parks have big celebrations – I went to a lovely one. Under irrepressible Mayor Luzhkov's direction, the city of Moscow paid for free treats for all in an area just off Red Square. Butter and Pancakes Week and Day are my favorite Russian holiday because they are sweet (double-entendre fully intended), Russian, and uncorrupted.

APRIL 20: HITLER'S BIRTHDAY (I am not kidding). The American Embassy periodically sends out security warnings to all Americans it has registered as resident in Russia. On April 18, we received a security alert from the embassy that Russian officials have given all the embassies a warning that "skinhead groups" of Nazi sympathizers are planning on celebrating Hitler's birthday by massing on the streets in areas known to be frequented by tourists. The Arbat, where I stroll every day, is one of the five places identified specifically as a likely venue. The skinheads, sentimental chaps that they are, apparently like to celebrate by attacking foreigners and are especially keen to beat up people of color. Several times in the past decade, their assaults have resulted in death.

MAY 1: LABOR DAY AND RUSSIAN ORTHODOX EASTER. Russians also celebrate Easter on a different schedule than do western Christians, and for the first time in this century, Russian Easter and Labor Day coincided in 2005. This may be an omen.

Labor Day is the day revered by the old defenders of the Soviet Union because, of course, it was the great holiday under Communism that commemorated the role of the working person. Officially known in Soviet times as The Day of International Workers' Solidarity, May Day was the day when the troops and tanks rumbled through Red Square and the Politburo viewed them proudly from Lenin's Tomb while western news organizations beamed the whole shebang to a fearful but fascinated capitalist world. Newly capitalist Russia has attempted to diminish Labor Day; last fall the government officially changed its name to The Day of Spring and Labor. It always did have a spring festival sense to it because so many Muscovites used the holiday to open up their summer cottages – their *dachas* – and begin the planting of their vegetable gardens. But understandably, old-line leftists and Soviets still revere the day and wish to use it as an occasion to make political statements.

At the other end of the political spectrum, Easter is the holiest day in the Christian church, and the Russian Orthodox Church is the most conservative institution in the country. It, too, wished to use the day for political statements. Who could imagine a scenario where fate would hand these two opposing persuasions the same day of the year for their great celebration?

I went to see the demonstration of the Communist sympathizers because it was well advertised in advance and I knew where to station myself. It seemed huge, boisterous, and angry although, of course, I could not tell what people were chanting nor could I read the signs. I did see several scuffles with police, a red sea of Soviet hammer and sickle flags, row after row of young people with scarves over their faces to obscure their identities, and similar rows of undisguised old men carrying red banners with pictures of Stalin on them. All told it was pretty darn impressive and a bit scary. The next day, the paper said that the most frequent banners read "Down with Putin," "Russia without Putin," and "Revolution," and that the scuffles had been provoked by the burning of pictures of Putin by demonstrators. The newspaper estimate for the crowd was fifty thousand, but it seemed larger to me.

It would be undignified for the Orthodox Church to mount demonstrations, but they had a proxy organization led by none other than His Honor, Mayor Luzhkov, do it for them. The United Russia Party, the party that supports Putin in the Duma, staged a much smaller rally under Mr. Luzhkov's sponsorship. I did not see this demonstration but apparently it drew less than ten thousand people and had little drama. A third and much smaller demonstration of civil libertarians organized boat cruises on the Moscow River, which seemed to me to be somewhat ill defined but innocuous.

All told, the city and country escaped Spring and Labor Day and Easter with a minimum of disruption. The *Moscow Times* reported that as many as 40 percent of Muscovites had left the city for the country, and preferred vegetables to political statements.

VICTORY DAY OVER GERMANY: MAY 9. President Putin decided to use the sixtieth anniversary of Russia's most heartfelt, emotional holiday of the year, Victory Day Over Germany, as a moment to showcase Russia's re-entry into the ranks of prosperous, respectable, stable world powers. Accordingly, he invited every world leader he could think of, and probably a few that his Kremlin advisors had to look up: Fifty-seven heads of state accepted his invitation, including President Bush, France's Chirac, Germany's Schroeder, Japan's Koizumi, and Ukraine's Yushchenko. On a sour note, two Baltic states indicated that they would not attend because they did not wish to celebrate the day when they say they passed from the domination of Nazi Germany to domination by Soviet Russia. This has infuriated virtually all Russians who look on the victory over Germany as a sacred event. The sixtieth anniversary was much bigger in Russia than the fiftieth was. In 1995 Russia was in near chaos and had not yet regained the post-Communist affection of most of a suspicious world. And no one could have counted on the emotional impact that the aging of the World War II veterans has had on the populations of all the countries that took part in that searing experience. Tom Brokaw's book *The Greatest Generation* has shown how much respect and affection this dying cohort of old warriors inspires in the United States. Increase that respect and affection exponentially for Russians, who positively revere the few surviving heroes.

Politics, of course, always and understandably tarnishes the holiest of moments, and genuine security concerns require every nation to wrap their celebrations in police blankets. Imagine, if you will, fifty-seven heads of state, including many of the most powerful in the world, arriving at airports, taking motor caravans to the central city, staying in hotels with their entourages–Bush's was estimated to be over 1,200–and moving around the city to various ceremonies. Nightmare city–and yet somehow Russia pulled it off without a hitch.

I say without a hitch, but that *is* the hitch: Russia did things that would have set American citizenry howling. For nearly two weeks before Victory

Day, Red Square was off limits to tourists or strollers; tens of thousands of police and military personnel fanned throughout the city core; and gunmen were ubiquitous on roofs. On the holiday weekend, all private hotel reservations were cancelled; helicopters buzzed everywhere in the sky; the two major airports that serve Moscow were shut down to all but official delegations; metro stations downtown were closed as were most city streets; and people were advised not to leave their flats if they lived near the city center. I went out shopping on May 7 and was stopped three times for lengthy document checks on a two-block outing. In short, the government made Moscow virtually off limits to its own inhabitants, and the celebrations were opened only to those with official invitations. Americans have grown much more accustomed to limits being placed on their freedom of movement since the events of 9/11, and everyone would acknowledge that President Putin's Victory Day party posed a challenge almost unparalleled in security history. Nevertheless, I do believe that an angry chorus of aggrieved citizens would have denounced similar measures imposed on Washington or New York.

Having been shut out of participation directly, however, did not mean that Russians did not have a chance personally to honor their war heroes. Wonderful posters of old men and women proudly wearing their medal-bedecked uniforms appeared in every little shop window in the city for three weeks before the holiday and many of them stayed up for weeks afterwards. I took part in an academic conference on World War II held in the Russian far eastern city of Khabarovsk and left Moscow by air on the evening of May 8. Getting me out of the city required extensive route planning, and I had to fly from a distant small airport that remained open. Khabarovsk proved to be an interesting place to observe Victory Day since the professors assembled needed no special protection—what terrorist would want to list an ivory-tower bombing on his or her vita? Khabarovsk's hotels were crowded with old soldiers who looked just like the people on the posters in Moscow, and whenever they walked into a restaurant or a lobby, other people stood up and applauded. I will confess to being teary-eyed every time I saw this.

Victory Day also has another function for Muscovites. They use it and the Spring and Labor Day holiday in the time-honored way many Americans use Memorial Day and Canadians use Victoria Day—as the time to open up their *dachas* and plant their vegetable gardens.

All told, Victory Day is a fine holiday but, of course, it will soon pass from shared experience to learned history and will undoubtedly lose a little of its hold on this country's emotions.

As I left, the country prepared for the newest official holiday, The Day of Russia, which commemorates the end of the Soviet Union. Preparations seemed to lack all enthusiasm and I believe that the future of The Day of Russia as a holiday does not look good. Like so much else in this country, the past and the present are colliding over holidays, and instead of allowing people to relax and celebrate joyfully some aspect of being alive, each new and old holiday seems to rub salt in the wounds of a society that is still trying to heal itself.

CHAPTER SIX

A Quick Guide to Present Politics
Why Russians Feel Misunderstood

Among my colleagues and students at Moscow State I have found substantial agreement on their views of some Russian leaders with whom we are all familiar. I realize that a near consensus in my sample does not mean unanimity across the board because my associates are urbane, highly educated, and privileged. Nevertheless, the agreement is far more than I would find among a similar sample of Americans or Canadians about their twentieth-century leaders. And the beliefs are surprising.

STALIN, the man we in the West have become accustomed to thinking of as nearly as evil as Hitler, has a much debated role in Russian history, but is held in high regard in two areas. First and foremost, as a great wartime leader, he is lionized in much the way the English *fête* Churchill as a man who reached down into his own inner strength and into the soul of the people to galvanize its resources and spirit in order to save the nation in the most perilous time of its history. Americans sustained fewer than a half million combat deaths in World War II; the Soviet Union lost somewhere between 23 and 27 million, depending on who is included in the count. Approximately one out of seven Soviets died from the war. Think of that—*one out of seven*. For certain age groups, the numbers were staggering. One of my students told me that her grandmother graduated from high school in June 1941, and that of the nineteen boys in her class, seventeen were killed in the war. The time between the end of the war and the 1960s is remembered as a generation of widows and the disabled. Memories of the war are omnipresent in the Russian mind today, and it is a much more frequent subject of discussion than it is in North America. Stalin saved the nation, it will be said by all, even though almost everyone acknowledges that the badly weakened officer corps at the beginning of the war was the result of his purges in the 1930s.

Second, everyone credits Stalin with the creation of industrial modern Russia and says that just because the Soviet Union and the Communist Party have collapsed – and perhaps it was good that it collapsed (this is more debated than westerners might think) – one should not think that the Russian Revolution and the Soviet years did not produce much good. The Bolsheviks came to power because most Russians supported them and neither the Czars nor their liberal-reformer successors in the early twentieth century were willing to make the needed changes. All of these statements of praise for Stalin come coupled with acknowledgments of the purges and the hardships caused by collectivization and industrialization. Most people have the attitude that "you can't make an omelet without breaking eggs," which I find a bit chilling, but also a bit hard to argue against. Almost everyone does say, however, that Stalin was a cruel man, and everyone does agree that he slid into gratuitous paranoia and anti-Semitism in his last few years. This, they say, is what led to the de-Stalinization of the late 1950s and 1960s, and most Russians now feel that the unequivocal reviling of Stalin was a mistake, and that his extraordinary accomplishments as well as his shortcomings should be appreciated.

Virtually everyone agrees that Stalin was the most influential Russian of the twentieth century. Even Stalin-haters do not gainsay his effect on history. Agreement breaks down, however, on how the balance-scales weigh on the good or bad side when assessing his influence. The distinguished sculptor Zurab Tsereteli, who had already become a political lightning rod through his designs of the new dome of Christ the Savior Cathedral and of the ridiculed Peter the Great statue, forced a public debate on the issue in 2005 when he presented the city of Yalta with a bronze statue of Stalin, Winston Churchill, and Franklin Roosevelt, commemorating their meeting there to plan for Europe's postwar reconstruction. After Khrushchev's denunciation of Stalin thousands of his statues had been torn down, and virtually none is left standing anywhere in Russia or the other countries of the former Soviet Union. Despite the extraordinary significance of the Yalta Conference, Yalta – now part of Ukraine – refused the statue because it did not want to do anything that

might be seen as publicly honoring Stalin. Tsereteli next offered his statue to Moscow as a free gift, and it too refused it. But Volgograd, the city
once known as Stalingrad, accepted it, and later this year the statue will
be erected.

Many Russian politicians undoubtedly would rather avoid taking a
stand on Stalin if they could, but public opinion and local politicians are
increasingly forcing the issue to the discomfort of national leaders. Members of the city legislature of Oryol, a large provincial urban center, sent a
petition to the Russian Duma that asked that they be allowed to name
streets, schools, and other landmarks after Stalin. The Oryol petition,
which was signed by thirty-three of the city's thirty-five elected deputies,
explicitly stated that the de-Stalinization movement was a mistake and
that Stalin should be historically rehabilitated as the father and savior of
modern Russia. Understandably, human rights activists everywhere are
aghast at the thought. The polar city of Mirny was even less politic than
Oryol: it restored its monument to Stalin in time for the May 9 Victory
Day celebration.

A well-known Russian proverb has been much cited over the continu-
ing controversy of Stalin's place in history. "In Russia, even the past is
unpredictable." This debate is far from over.

A few weeks after I wrote the above, on the week preceding the Victory
Day celebrations, a three-sided monument with portraits of Churchill,
Roosevelt and Stalin was quietly unveiled to little or no controversy in a
small park outside of the New Opera House in Moscow. The May 4 *Moscow
Times* quoted President Putin as saying "it would be silly to ignore" Stalin's
leadership role in the war, and most Russians seem to agree, regardless of
their political commitments. A representative survey of 1,600 Russians
conducted by respected pollster Dmitry Polikanov reported that 58 percent of the respondents attributed victory in World War II to Stalin's military genius.

NIKITA KRUSHCHEV, the bald, smiley, personable little guy who infamously debated Richard Nixon at a Moscow trade show – the so-called
"kitchen debate" because it took place in a showroom of new appliances –
has not fared as well in Russian memory as Americans might expect.
Khrushchev became the first Soviet leader to visit the United States,

where he toured farms in Iowa with President Eisenhower and banged his shoe in protest on his desk at the United Nations. His antics and carica- tured charm made him memorable to my generation of Americans, and almost endearing, if an American could think of a Soviet Communist as such. But Russians downplay his influence because he was not in power long enough – a mere nine years – to have stamped an era with anything distinctive. Khrushchev is most remembered for a type of building named after him. Khrushchoby are five-story apartment buildings that were built by the tens of thousands and on the cheap across Russia in the 1960s. They were intended to be used only temporarily for a generation to relieve a dreadful housing shortage. They are all the same, are often built in clusters of ten to thirty, contain three-room, shabby little apartments, and were a great benefit to millions of young Russians who could move out of their parents' homes and start a nuclear household. They are virtu- ally all still in use today, although some are being replaced. So Khrushchev has become an apartment block to the popular mind.

Khrushchev had one other acknowledged major effect on Russia and that did derive from his trip to the United States. He was so impressed by the high yields that American farmers got from their corn crops that he ordered Soviet agricultural planners to investigate corn's suitability for Russian agriculture and the result was a massive increase in the cultivation of corn by Russia's cooperative farms.

Americans also remember Khrushchev for his role in the Cuban mis- sile crisis, which looms in the West as the most perilous moment of the Cold War. It has no such place in the Russian mind and is perceived as a relatively minor event.

The diminution of Khrushchev's role in Soviet history is best symbol- ized by where he is buried – not in the Kremlin Wall. He lies in Novode- vichy Cemetery, the number-two burial ground in the country. I have heard many Russians say that this is a disgrace and that it only happened because Khrushchev's successors wanted to legitimize their own purge that forced him to resign. If he died today, Khrushchev might well rate the Kremlin Wall for eternity.

LEONID BREZHNEV, who assumed joint power along with Alexey Kosygin at Khrushchev's ouster in 1964, went on within a few years to be the primary leader and stayed in power until 1980, despite being dreadfully ill for at least the last five years. Brezhnev inspires little personal commentary – he seemed to be largely colorless, a giant bear of a man who always appeared old – but Russians associate his era with the best of times in the twentieth century. If there was a golden age of Soviet Communism, it would be the Brezhnev era: no major wars or internal revolts (until the Afghan crisis near the end of his era); no need to undergo any projects such as collectivization, which was achieved at the cost of great human sacrifice; and no major defense buildup to sap the resources of the economy during this era of détente with the United States. During the Brezhnev years, Soviet citizens enjoyed their first real taste of western-style consumer goods, most were adequately housed, and – although they did not enjoy any semblance of political freedom – they did not have large contingents of their fellow citizens consigned to the gulags. It was the happiest time in memory. In the mid-1970s, when Moscow received the 1980 Olympics, hopes were high of a bright future. Understandably, Russians hold Brezhnev in quiet but unaffectionate high regard.

The Brezhnev era came crashing down with the Soviet-Afghan War, the American boycott of the Olympics, the Reagan-era denunciation of the Soviets as an "evil empire," the new arms race of the early 1980s, and the exposed inefficiencies in the Soviet systems of production. But Russians by and large do not blame Brezhnev – he was old, tired, and ill – nor do they give his two short-lived successors, Yuri Andropov and Konstantin Chernenko, who each were in power just slightly longer than one year, either credit or blame for the world-shaking changes that were about to come.

MIKHAIL GORBACHEV, the man whom we in the West have come to associate with the ending of an oppressive empire and brutal regime and the beginning of a new wonderful era of Russian history, is widely disliked in Russia. I had assumed that he was much less popular at home than in the West because I knew that he failed to be elected to office after the democratic constitution of 1993 was adopted. I also assumed that he probably was seen as always kissing up to western leaders. Gorbachev received less than 1 percent of the vote when he ran for president in 1996. He is regarded as being so anxious to please the West and the Communist Party and everyone else that he simply had no backbone – "he is no Joe Stalin," I could almost always hear people want to say. He ended the Soviet state and Soviet economy, but had no plan for anything new to replace it. Gorbachev turned the country over to western professors who had no realistic ideas, and to gangsters who stole the factories, mines, resources, and wealth that had been accumulated by the people's sweat and sacrifice.

At present, Gorbachev is a joke among many Russians and has no influence whatsoever in the public arena over policy debates. Whenever Gorbachev makes any pronouncement on public policy, all Russians of every political stripe smile and say the same thing: that he is trying to increase his speaking fees and invitations in western Europe and the United States. Although he once was a man of power, Gorbachev is now regarded as one of those media celebrities who are primarily famous for being famous.

BORIS YELTSIN. Russians are a little kinder to Boris Yeltsin, but they also assign him much blame for the morass the country now faces economically. As an opposition leader and as a foe of the late Soviet state, Yeltsin showed much talent and courage but as a leader, he seemed better disposed towards tearing things down than building them up. All Russians remember with pride and affection Yeltsin's role in ending the coup mounted against Gorbachev in August 1991; but they also remember with greater embarrassment Yeltsin's frequent public drunkenness and they especially are horrified by his out-of-control behavior on his trip to visit President Clinton in the United States.

Yeltsin also shares with Gorbachev much of the blame for the debacle of privatization. If Gorbachev had no plans and fiddled while the Russian economy burned, Yeltsin acted precipitously and turned over the Russian-held assets from the former Soviet Union too quickly and too cheaply to a small coterie of hustlers and sharpies who flattered, deceived, and supported him in the presidential election of 1996 when his future seemed threatened at the polls. The new "oligarchs," as Russia's robber barons are ubiquitously called, have their origins in the Yeltsin years but most people attribute their emergence more to Yeltsin's drunkenness and inattention rather than to willful corruption on his part. Thus Yeltsin receives as much blame as Gorbachev does, but is held in greater personal affection. Only among diehard Communists is Yeltsin roundly disliked; they revile him as the man who ended the Soviet Union.

Many urban legends and tales swirl about Yeltsin in the popular culture. He died in April 2007 as this book was in its final rewrite, but the fact that he lived so long seems astounding and was frequently explained to me in two ways: first, that Yeltsin died shortly after leaving office and that the person who appeared to be Yeltsin from then until 2007 was in reality one of the doubles that he had used as security decoys. Everyone agrees that he had several of these. And second, Yeltsin went to China for a lengthy medical treatment that is often talked about in mysterious terms: something strange was done to him by herbalists practicing ancient Chinese techniques. Yeltsin withdrew virtually entirely from the political arena after leaving office, but of course he did arrange for the election of his successor, Vladimir Putin, by plucking Putin from relative obscurity and appointing him prime minister – the fifth prime minister of Yeltsin's eight years in office. Shortly after appointing Putin, Yeltsin resigned in late 1999, which made Putin the acting president at the time of the 2000 election. Without the advantage of incumbency, Putin would very likely not have been elected.

VLADIMIR PUTIN. Although he owes his initial election to Yeltsin, Putin has spent his entire presidency trying to clean up the mess that Yeltsin made of privatization.

Throughout my stay in Russia, Presidents George Bush and Vladimir Putin lectured each other in the Russian and European news. Bush started it, or more precisely, Secretary of State Condoleezza Rice started it a few weeks before the February 2005 European summit, which President Bush attended. In an infamous (at least to Russians) statement at a mid-February press conference, Secretary Rice said that although President Bush had grave concerns over Russia's backsliding towards authoritarianism, Russia would not be "punished." Secretary Rice is an extraordinary American of unquestioned accomplishment and ability and much to be admired, but the quotient of gall required to make a statement like that leaves me breathless. Moreover, it did not strike me as very good diplomacy at a time when the Bush administration was trying to cozy up to a Europe angry at America over the Iraq War.

The nub, however, of Secretary Rice's and President Bush's criticism of President Putin's alleged backsliding is as follows. The central government under Putin has: (1) cancelled several elections of state governors and appointed its own substitutes; (2) seized several privately owned companies and brought them under the government's control; (3) curtailed the civil liberties of many dissidents; and (4) restricted media freedom. All told, Rice, Bush, much of the political establishment in both the Republican and Democratic parties, and the Western media decry these changes as moving back towards the evil days of Soviet repression.

All four charges are true, but they signify no such slide back towards Soviet authoritarianism. If any of these programs were being implemented in the United States, they would pose an unparalleled challenge to American democracy, but Russia is not the United States. Most Russians I speak to about Putin are very critical of him for other parts of his government's programs but most support 1, 2, and 3 above. Most do not support point 4.

THE CANCELING OF STATE ELECTIONS. As one student said to me with a wisdom beyond her years, democracy is not always a simple matter. For starters, Russia is not a federal system, and elections were not held in the eighty-nine official regions in Russia until the country adopted a new Constitution in 1993. Thus regional elections are recent, and in a sense were an experiment proposed by the central government. Why after gifting these elections did the Kremlin under Putin revoke some of them, and why are people not outraged? I would be the first to mount the barricades if any president, Republican or Democrat, set aside New Hampshire's elected governor and dispatched a Washington friend to go to Concord and run the state. People in Russia are not furious at this revocation of the gift of electoral rights because they believe that in most or all of these cases, criminal or corrupt elements have seized control of the elections and are using their control of local governorships for nefarious purposes. The United States had extraordinary corruption at the municipal level in the late nineteenth century; multiply these machine-boss regimes by ten and throw in shipments of Kalashnikovs, and you approximate the situation in Russia under which elections have been suspended. Neither did President Putin summarily impose these suspensions. The Duma, Russia's parliament, authorized the president to proceed as he is doing. Nor does Putin directly name governors; he proposes nominees to regional parliaments who can accept or reject them. Much investigation preceded all of the decisions to set aside some elections, and the public generally supports the central government because the public fears a return to the catastrophic corruption and violence of the 1990s more than it fears a loss of local autonomy. The public is making a reasonable choice.

Democracy is not always a simple matter, and it does take many forms.

THE SEIZURE OF PRIVATE COMPANIES. Get ready for more of this in Ukraine, where the government presided over by Victor Yuschchenko, the new president adored by the Western media, is feeling pressure to do the same thing. Governments are doing it because of the horrible mistakes made during the earlier pell-mell rush towards privatization. The Yeltsin governments, out of good intentions, wanted to divest the government from its ownership of the factories and resources of the country because it thought—and properly so—that the private sector would be more efficient at managing them for the good of all. Fine. But the accumulated industrial capital built by three generations of sacrifice and sweat was sold for a song—often for no money at all but for loans—to a relatively small number of investors who used bribery, violence, and even murder to get their hands on these assets. These people were not the MBAS or CEOS of western Europe or the United States, who would manage their enterprises for the good of shareholders; they were often organized cabals of criminals who got control of the physical, hard resources of the Russian heartland and now exploited them for straightforward greed.

And yet worse: the futures of the next generations of Russians were also compromised because the same types of people grabbed leases on the oil, gas, and mineral resources of the vast Russian East. So heartland and hinterland went from being badly managed by the Communist Party to being badly exploited by a nexus of corrupt, exploitative "oligarchs" who are pretty darn close to a criminal party. Just as Putin and his government inherited this situation from the Yeltsin government, so too the present Ukrainian government inherited a similar situation from the Kuchma government: sober-minded reformers in both Russia and Ukraine feel they have no choice but to void some of the deals that resulted in the most egregious pillaging of the public purse. Once again, a majority of Russians agree. The ones who do not and are inflaming the U.S. Congress through their testimony invariably are indicted business-men who are trying to save their loot by hiding behind a self-serving smoke screen of free-enterprise rhetoric.

Most of the time that I was in Russia, the trial of Mikhail Khodorkovsky and Platon Lebedev played out as big news both there and in the West. Khodorkovsky, formerly head of Yukos, the giant Russian oil company, was the richest person in Russia in 2004 and a poster boy for the new Russian oligarchs, tycoons, capitalists, or robber barons, depending on your choice of words. Lebedev is one of his major associates and also a billion-aire. The two are charged with tax evasion in the billions, business fraud, forgery, and, in general, dreadful white-collar crimes that bilked the Russ-ian people and government out of an unbelievable amount of money.

The trial can be interpreted in contrasting partisan ways, but I believe a rough consensus exists among honest people and that both partisan views have a little truth to them coupled with a lot of overstatement.

In the West and in Russia among anti-Putin forces, the trial is por-trayed as a throwback to Soviet centralization and persecution. According to these viewpoints, Putin and his advisors wanted to renationalize the oil industry and eliminate Khodorkovsky as a potential presidential candi-date in 2008, so they trumped up these charges and have conducted a kangaroo court in which the two defendants had no fair chance of pre-senting a reasonable defense. Russian business people overseas have been pounding this interpretation out to a steady drumbeat.

Among Putin supporters, the line simply is that these two men and Yukos are no heroes of the new capitalism but rather have shown a cal-lousness and greed rather like Enron's in the United States, and they were indulged – perhaps even encouraged – to flout the law by the Yeltsin administration in return for their support. Their trial is fair and should be an example to others, Putin's partisans argue, that the privatization process does not exist merely to enrich the oligarchs, but must also be law-ful and respectful of due process and the interests of the Russian people.

Virtually everyone I know or heard interviewed who was not an associ-ate of the two, or a concerned oligarch, believes that the two are guilty of most of the accusations against them. Okay. But almost everyone goes on to say that the Yukos executives were singled out – and unfairly so – because Khodorkovsky does have political ambitions and did dare to challenge Putin and the Kremlin. Had Khodorkovsky publicly supported Putin and played ball with Kremlin programs, had he agreed to stay out of politics, some *quid pro quo* would have been worked out, and these drastic charges would not have been instituted – a statement of back taxes due and a bill being paid would have done the trick. Almost everyone I know also believes the judiciary is not independent and, regardless of the evidence or the defense, the two men had no chance of being acquitted.

So in a real sense, the trial suggests the old "a pox on both their houses" judgment is accurate. Khodorkovsky cheated the country but is being singled out for prosecution (persecution) because he is a political rival. And the country – poor Russia – loses. First, it does make outside business people understandably wary about investing in a country where the government can so easily seize assets and manipulate justice. Second, it does – quite unfairly, but once again understandably – add grist to the mill of those who want to portray Putin as a neo-Communist or neo-Stalinist. And, third, the newspaper pictures shown day after day of Khodorkovsky and Lebedev being kept in large cages in the courtroom could not have been more unfortunate for the image of Russia abroad.

The trial ended in late May after months, including an eleven-day long reading of the verdict by the three judges who alternated turns to preserve their voices while Khodorkovsky and Lebedev doodled on sketchpads in their cages. The sentence: nine years at hard labor for each man.

The trial has been ruinous for everyone's interests. Western journalists' coverage of it makes Putin appear to be anti-business and anti-free market, but nothing could be further from the truth. Think back to the first decades of the twentieth century when the Progressive movement, led by the Republican Theodore Roosevelt and the Democrat Woodrow Wilson, attacked the oligarchs of American industry. They did so not because they were anti-business but because they wanted business to be responsive to the public good. Small business people applauded the Progressives because small business was being swallowed up by a few brutes at the top of the economic food chain. America's oligarchs had been destroying honest competition and the free market, and Roosevelt and Wilson wanted to tame their oppressive power so small business had a chance to compete. This is exactly what Putin is trying to do, and small business people in Russia generally support him, as do most Russians. Business of any sort also thrives on stability in society, and Putin has brought a much-needed order to the country. Alas, more order is still needed, but as a historian I could not help noticing the same parallel to American society when the Progressives also sought to bring order to a United States social order that had been devastated by industrialization.

CRACKING DOWN ON DISSIDENTS. A month after I arrived in Moscow, President Putin dedicated a monument to commemorate the first anniversary of a terrorist attack on a metro stop that left 45 people dead. In the same year, terrorists had commandeered a Moscow movie theater and killed over a hundred people. As I write this in early 2007, parents of the over 300 children killed in the September 2004 Beslan terrorist attack south of Moscow continue to demand a full investigation into how such a tragedy could happen. Russia, as does the United States, considers itself to be at war with terrorists. For this reason, most Russians that I know support Putin's willingness to tolerate some intrusions into the citizenry's recently acquired civil liberties. I do not support him in this–not that he cares–but President Putin is using the exact same defense that President Bush and the U.S. Congress used to pass the Patriot Act, which also curtails civil liberties. I do not support the Patriot Act either, but the reasoning for both men is the same. Putin can get more public support than Bush can for their similar acts, because Russia has much less of a tradition of civil liberty than the United States. But in neither case do we see a complete abandonment of legal protections for most citizens. Instead we see two frightened countries and two leaders willing to sacrifice a little freedom for what they hope is enough extra protection to make their compromise a worthwhile bargain.

RESTRICTED MEDIA FREEDOM. This seems indefensible to me, and I know very few people who support President Putin on this matter. Everyone says that although security concerns in Chechnya are given as the reason, the true cause is to spare the government criticism, and I believe that this is true. But let us not overstate the problem. Moscow papers are daily filled with criticisms of the Putin government and all the recent ongoing anti-government demonstrations are thoroughly covered in the media. And, of course, ongoing street demonstrations take place weekly. The government is trying to control the press less through censorship and repression, and more through asserting its own version of news stories through government-controlled media. Once again, Putin is doing this at the same time that scandals have enveloped the Bush administration over monies paid by the Department of Education to news columnists to support the No Child Left Behind Act, and over monies paid by the American military to Iraqi journalists to print favorable stories about the Iraq War.

Democracy is not perfect – in Russia or in the United States.

After enduring first Secretary Rice and then President Bush's public lecturing of him as if he were an errant schoolboy, President Putin struck back. He is a tough customer. After his defense based on the arguments outlined above, President Putin expressed the fear that the United States was trying to isolate Russia from the world community, much as it tried to do through "containment" in the Cold War. Bringing NATO to the Russian border is obviously the most overt sign of a Russian insecurity sensitized by a great deal of historical reality. And a good offense is always the best defense. Putin has repeatedly lashed out at the United States for its human rights violations at Guantanamo Bay in Cuba, in the Iraqi jail scandals, and in its tortured definition of the concept of torture. Tit for tat.

The truth is that Putin is no pushover and has more political moxy than Gorbachev and more discipline than Yeltsin. He clearly is the most important leader to emerge in this part of the world since the Soviet empire ended, and his vision competes and cooperates alternately with the Stalinesque legacy of strength, security, and repression. Ironically, when President Bush in his first term seemed to find that he and Putin had compatible souls, he may have been closer to the truth on many aspects of their governments than he realized. Each president is obsessed with security because each president has seen firsthand the awful power of criminal terrorism, and each of the two leaders seems to let his fears override other scruples.

And each of the two leaders has stirred up precisely the same hornet's nest at home by attacking the benefits being extended to the elderly in society. Once again, a similar problem underlies the common response. A demographic bulge of old people faces both countries, and as President

Bush mounted the first real attack on Social Security since it was created, President Putin replaced free transportation, medical benefits, and energy with an inadequate cash payment. Putin reaped the whirlwind on this and retreated, at least temporarily, as President Bush also has retreated in his efforts to privatize some Social Security investments as the Iraq War consumes all the energy of his administration.

As all Russians – both Putin supporters and detractors – reminded me, when we try to explain President Putin's conduct, we should not forget that he made his career as a KGB agent, and thus security concerns and statism come naturally to his personality. He does indeed have the spy's temperament and demeanor. He plays his cards close to his chest and seems to enjoy watching others more than being watched. In a state-of-the-union address given two weeks before his grand Victory Day party planned for Moscow on May 9, 2005, Putin outlined his vision for Russia's future – in order to have it on the record before Western leaders showed up to give another lecture on Russia's shortcomings. Putin made three main points that should be carefully considered by political critics because they have guided his entire presidency:

1. Russia will pursue a democratic future, but will define democracy by its own criteria. "I consider the development of Russia as a free state to be the main political and ideological task," he argued, and the country must "become a free society of free people." But, he continued, "as a sovereign country, Russia is capable and will itself define the terms and conditions for progress along this way." Read this statement to mean in code: "Butt out of Russia's business, Messrs. Bush, Blair, and Chirac. Our history and present needs require different democratic solutions from ones based on American, British, and French history." Putin then went on to identify specific security concerns that could not be tolerated in the name of freedom.

2. Secondly, Putin argued that Russia would continue to be a major force in bringing stability and promoting peace in the central Asian republics that have emerged from the wreckage of the Soviet Union. In this regard, he issued a statement rather reminiscent of the United States when it issued the Monroe Doctrine in the 1820s. As the new American republic argued that it had a special interest in the affairs of

its own backyard, so too Putin is arguing that any sense of *realpolitik* must accept that Russia has a special interest in its immediate neighbors. Big powers behave that way with little powers that are nearby.

3. And finally, Putin tried to make clear that his government's prosecution of some of the oligarchs for corruption was not anti-business, but merely an honest attempt to eliminate the grossest of corruptions that had accompanied privatization in the Yeltsin years. Although Putin owes his initial election to the presidency to Boris Yeltsin's anointing him as his successor, he harshly criticized Yeltsin in this address and said that under Yeltsin's shoddy stewardship, "poverty became the norm." Once again, this message is aimed at Western leaders and critics as much or perhaps more so than at Russians. Although some business people may genuinely fear that Putin is overstepping the appropriate boundaries of a free market, as we suggested above, many others support him because of his emphasis on the need for stability. Business works best in a peaceful country of contented citizens and predictable circumstances.

All told, Putin's state of the union address was remarkably strong politically and rang true to everyone I know who commented on it. Surprisingly, Boris Yeltsin, who received such harsh criticism that he might well consider Putin an ingrate, publicly stated that he admired and supported the speech. People did complain that Putin was short on specifics and that they would like to have seen the rhetoric tied more closely to concrete proposals.

AMERICANS AND PRESIDENT BUSH, RUSSIANS AND PRESIDENT PUTIN

One of my students made an interesting observation about Americans and Russians, and the students in all three of my seminars agreed almost unanimously. Americans, he said, all feel responsible for their president's political and personal conduct – that he is a reflection upon them. Thus, American professors, who usually do not support President Bush's foreign policy, feel a need to apologize for it. If the president acts inappropriately, Americans feel embarrassed by his behavior. This, the student said, is a sign of democracy – that right or wrong, like or dislike, Americans feel invested in the president as a visible sign of their own personal identity. Russians, he said, feel little such personal involvement with President Putin or with any leader. He and other leaders make decisions or take stands that the students may support or oppose, but none of them feel a close connection to leaders; and certainly, average Russian citizens do not personalize their relationship with leaders. If Putin acts badly, Putin acts badly, but his behavior does not reflect on most Russians' own sense of self. Russians tend to identify more with distant historical figures than with living people.

I have been trying to sort out whether I think the above is a good or a bad thing. I think the students are right; certainly I do feel a personal responsibility for the American president's political behavior and stands, and especially so when I travel overseas, because although only Americans elect the president, he serves as a leader of extraordinary consequence for the rest of the world, which does not have a say in choosing him. Average Russians' emotional detachment from their leaders can certainly be viewed as a sign of maturity. I have no doubt that too many American and Canadian leaders are elected because we just gosh-darn like them and like the idea that they represent us. We want our presidents and prime ministers to be our friends, and that may be a bit silly. Alternatively, the Russian detachment can be seen as a sign of paralyzing cynicism and apathy, by which citizens do not think their leaders are interested in the lives of average voters, so why should citizens be interested in theirs? Somehow, I think our emotional and personal investment in a president's image is good for democracy, but I do also think that it does look – and probably is – naïve.

Where is a new Tocqueville when we need him to help us better understand how Americans can still be the blushing brides of democracy after more than two hundred years in the political bedroom?

As President Putin's two terms in office come closer to an end – he is constitutionally forbidden from a third term – his popularity has grown massively. Curiously enough, many Russians do seem to be identifying with him despite their avowed cynicism. Partly his popularity stems from Russia's surging economy in 2006 and 2007 brought on by the worldwide boom in oil prices. Even more importantly, Putin's strength in reasserting Russia's role in international matters has earned him the respect of upwards of three-quarters of his countrymen – a figure that dwarfed the dwindling popularity of Prime Minister Blair and President Chirac as they were respectively replaced by Gordon Brown and Nicolas Sarkozy, and also dwarfs that of President Bush as he enters the lame-duck phase of his administration. Putin's steadfastness and domestic prestige seem to rise in inverse proportion to Bush's plummeting popularity at home and vilification abroad. As the wars in Iraq and Afghanistan moved from bad to worse in 2007, as Iran's and Venezuela's presidents humiliatingly twitted the U.S. at the United Nations, and as the Democrats took control of the Congress and took aim at the presidency, Putin mounted a stunning verbal counteroffensive that turned the rhetorical tables on his Western critics.

In a February 2007 speech to 250 diplomats, scholars, international businesspeople and military leaders from more than forty countries attending the Munich Conference on Security Policy, Putin unloaded on the United States in a diatribe that paid Bush and Rice back in spades for their hectoring of him in previous years. His preface presaged a biting attack when he thanked the conference for providing him an opportunity to speak in language that "avoid[ed] excessive politeness and ... roundabout, pleasant but empty diplomatic terms." NATO's expansion to Russia's border provoked Putin's anger specifically, but he expanded this aggressive affront to Russian security into a denunciation of the American "unipolar model" that replaced the old superpower model of the Cold War era. "The United States has overstepped its national borders in every way," Putin argued, and shows it daily in "the economic, political, cultural, and educational policies it imposes on other nations. Well, who likes this? Who is happy about this?" In Russia, he argued, "we are constantly being taught about democracy. But for some reason, those who teach us do not want to learn themselves."

Uniformly, American newspapers have misconstrued Putin's extraordinarily frank speech as a throwback to the Soviet era and part of his attempt to ratchet up a new Cold War relationship with the United States. Nothing could be further from the truth. Putin is merely voicing what almost all Russians want to tell the United States, namely that they should stop trying to isolate Russia, stop meddling in its internal affairs, and stop promoting hostile governments in adjacent countries. Moreover, Putin used this opportunity to further assert Russian international influence by saying without guile or nuance what much of the world believes – the

United States has been acting like an undiplomatic bull in the global china shop. It must instead respect the opinions, counsel, and policy of other nations. American hubris over Middle East policy, Iraq, Afghanistan, the war on terror, and Russia's alleged shortcomings gave Putin a poetic moment late in his presidency that may well be his valedictory. Putin's commanding presence and the absence of any serious opposition at the moment make it likely that he will be able virtually to appoint his own successor in 2008 by simply announcing his support for one of the two leading candidates, both of whom serve in his cabinet.

When Putin lambasted the United States' heavy-handed unilateralism, he pointed to many international flash points that domestic critics of the Bush administration also cite as egregious examples of American hubris. Examples close to home, however, anger Russians the most. In particular, they have been infuriated by American perceptions of three widely hailed "revolutions" in former parts of the Soviet Union – the "Rose Revolution" in Georgia in 2003, the "Orange Revolution" in Ukraine in 2004 and 2005, and the "Tulip Revolution" in Kyrgyzstan in 2005. All of these have been portrayed by Europe and the United States as courageous uprisings of freedom-loving peoples who wish to sweep out remnants of corrupt old Soviet-era regimes. And, indeed, to a substantial degree this view is accurate. On the other hand, however, these revolutions can be seen (and are seen by most Russians) as anti-Russian coups fomented by Western nations who are using local unrest to create governments that will isolate Russia from the West. These coups are deeply worrisome to Russians who resent what they regard as meddling by western Europe and the United States in an area of the world where Russia must be the preeminent power.

As in the Domino Theory used by the West to justify its containment policy towards Communism during the Cold War, Russia fears that more anti-Russian dominoes may soon be falling. And indeed, unrest that could lead to coups is everywhere here in the new republics. Most of these republics are politically corrupt, and none of their governments will ever win an award for democracy and honesty, but their tottering is a sign of the colossal insecurity in central Asia and the Caspian regions. Russia feels very much threatened by this instability and by the West's interference in areas that Russians regard as geographically and strategically belonging to their own sphere of influence.

Most American politicians, both Republican and Democratic, support peaceful regime change in the former Soviet republics of central Asia, but the product of newly found democratic aspirations may not be to most Americans' liking. Almost assuredly, Islamic republics will replace the old Soviet regimes. The best that the West can hope for is moderation. Situations will arise in central Asia that are similar to the one produced by the Palestinians' election of Hamas: the people will choose some governments that the West will not like.

Most of us in the West were aware of the extraordinary circumstances of the elections held in Ukraine in fall 2004, in which Victor Yuschchenko, the reform-minded, pro-Western challenger to President Leonid Kuchma's handpicked successor, was allegedly poisoned with dioxin during the campaign. Yuschchenko survived and won in a second effort after courts overturned the first election as corrupt, but the dioxin left this man, who had movie-star good looks, with a disfigured face. It is widely believed that Russian FSB agents (the replacement for the KGB) helped Kuchma's minions carry out the poisoning, but at this date no one knows for sure who did the deed and people are not above saying that Yuschchenko's friends did it to discredit their enemies. What is known, however, is that political assassinations and murders occur too often in this tough part of the world. The situation in Ukraine was not as exceptional as we might think; police chiefs, opposition leaders, journalists, and legislators are killed with alarming frequency.

Nothing has brought the horror of Russian political violence more forcefully to the world's attention than the assassination in 2007 of Anna Politkoyskaya, a journalist renowned for her fierce criticism of Putin's government, and the ghastly radium poisoning of Alexander Litvinenko, a London-based Russian dissident who lived in the shadowy world of information trading. Critics of Putin and his government were quick to blame the Kremlin for both murders, as did Litvinenko himself from his deathbed. Both assassinations have been used to ratchet up the charges that Russia is reverting to its Soviet past. Supporters of Putin and most Russians – but not all – dismiss these charges as silly and argue that the Russian leadership would have to be idiots not to know that these public, violent murders would do them more harm than good. As with Yuschchenko's poisoning in Ukraine, the deaths of Politkoskaya and Litvinenko have become fodder for a debate between Putin's supporters and opponents – and, of course, the entire debate takes place amidst a complete absence of reliable knowledge.

There is no debate, however, over the proposition that these assassinations and revolutions and upheavals in general reinforce the judgment that the region of the former Soviet Union is a violent place and likely to get more violent. Diplomacy towards Russia and its neighbors requires more than simple lectures based on a shallow understanding of the momentous changes that are overtaking people, most of whom wish to be our friends and also wish to have a market economy and a standard of living much like our own. If we want to be friends with Russia and its neighbors, and if we do support their aspirations for better lives, we should begin by acknowledging the complexity of the choices that Russians and other former Soviets face in the world of 2007 and beyond; we should not reduce these choices to black-and-white alternatives of neo-Soviet centralism versus free markets; we should not humiliate the Russian people or leadership by public rebukes; we should acknowledge that Russia has a special interest in central Asia and in other areas on its borders; and we should look at our own history to gain a full appreciation of how difficult the business of making a democratic country can be.

History Is Heavy

History weighs heavily on Russia. All nations have histories of triumphs and tragedies—all peoples have memories of shared joys passed down through the generations in families, proverbs, tales, songs, and books; all peoples inherit sorrows from the past that seep into their marrow and cannot be forgotten, even though they are usually more felt than remembered.

History seems to have been a bit tough on Russians, however, and given them more sadness than it has to most people. There are no glorious epochs to be collectively remembered with unambiguous pride—no Elizabethan or Victorian Englands, no Revolutionary Americas or heroic westward movements. We know, of course, that most of Elizabethan England lived in dark, squalid poverty and never saw a Shakespearean play, and we know that a greater percentage of Americans died during the Revolution than in any other war the country fought. But history's true impact is not always measured by reality. A majority of English and American citizens have collective memories that evoke vibrant, unabashedly celebratory images. Russians do not.

Russians celebrate their Czars and put their clothes and carriages in museums, but all Russians know that serfdom existed here until 1861, and that even after they were freed, peasants were ground to unhappy early deaths between the millstones of ignorance, disease, starvation, battle, poverty, and oppression. Many Russians take pride in the Russian Revolution and the heroic leap to industrialism, but no historical amnesia can make those events into happy times. Victory over Nazi Germany and fascism in "The Great Patriotic War" is a cause for even more pride, but here the grim impress of history is yet more obvious: one-seventh of Russia died

149

in World War II. And, finally, whatever one thinks of the Soviet Union during the Cold War era—a heroic attempt to create a true worker's republic, or a left-wing fascist repressive regime—nothing in the popular imagination can transform the last half-century into the Gay Nineties or Roaring Twenties with a rollicking, folk-cultural memory of good times.

Russia's past—or at least its public past—seems darker than that of most of the other European nations and the European tradition. The greatest historical triumphs felt by most Russians have come from resisting the invasions of outsiders, and these triumphs always came with too high a price to be cause for anything but the most somber of celebrations. This dark history that is so personally felt by all Russians is the key to understanding this country in the early twenty-first century. If one adds Russia's long historical grayness to the dazzling, immediate adrenalin of the privatization process, many of the paradoxes that greeted me in Moscow become more understandable.